Praise for *The Best New True Crime Sto...*
Unsolved Crimes & Mysteries

"Haunting and heartbreaking, *The Best New True Crime Stories: Unsolved Crimes & Mysteries* lives up to its title, and is a must-read for true crime aficionados. It's an ambitious collection of unsolved mysteries, spanning the globe and time—from France in the Roaring Twenties to Los Angeles in the 1960s to the Appalachian Trail in the 1990s, and beyond. The authors skillfully shed new light on long-forgotten murders, chronical a baffling and brazen art heist, and lay bare the systemic and societal failures in each case. But most of all, the authors honor the victims. Because maybe, just maybe, these renewed accounts will spawn new clues that will provide answers to grieving families, and perhaps even justice. I can't stop thinking about these stories, and I highly recommend."

—**Alex Finlay**, author of *Every Last Fear* and *The Night Shift*

"Ever since reading Megan Abbott's *The Song is You,* I can't get enough of Jean Spangler, so I was thrilled to see the bizarre 1949 disappearance of the Hollywood bit actress turn up in Mitzi Szereto's latest collection of unsolved true crimes. If you love history and mystery, you'll love this book."

—**David Bushman**, author of *Murder at Teal's Pond: Hazel Drew and the Mystery That Inspired Twin Peaks*

"An unusually moving read. I was struck by the compassion and sensitivity with which the murders were described, as each of the authors felt a personal sympathy with and even a connection to the case."

—**Linda Stratmann**, author of thirty true crime and crime fiction books, including her new series featuring a young Sherlock Holmes

"Quality literature always leaps from the pages when professional true crime writers dip quills into ink. This book is no exception. A great compilation of gut-wrenching cases giving 'reader involvement and participation:' the authors 'talk to the reader' not 'at the reader,' which is a style I encourage and thoroughly endorse. Well laid out. Dedicated research. This is a must-read book for all those interested in true crime."

—**Christopher Berry-Dee**, criminologist; christopherberrydee.com

"Author and editor extraordinaire Mitzi Szereto has assembled an outstanding group of leading authors from throughout the world for this incredible collection—*The Best New True Crime Stories: Unsolved Crimes & Mysteries*. A truly fantastic anthology!"

—**Dan Zupansky**, author and host of *True Murder*

Praise for Mitzi's Other Collections

"Readers can't get enough true crime and here comes another winner in Mitzi Szereto's *The Best New True Crime Stories: Partners in Crime.* Gathering stories from some of the world's best writers, Szereto puts together another page-turning collection, telling true crime tales of the wicked, wild, and wonderful. You'll love this book and the stories of devious partnerships that ended in mayhem and murder!"

—**Bob Batchelor**, cultural historian and author of *The Bourbon King: The Life and Crimes of George Remus, Prohibition's Evil Genius*

"True crime fans hungering for juicy tales of hot-blooded murder will gobble up the offerings in this irresistibly page-turning collection."

—**Harold Schechter**, author of *Hell's Princess: The Mystery of Belle Gunness, Butcher of Men*

"Szereto and her contributors' dark stories and clean writing styles combine for a gripping read. Wonderful!"

—**Liza Rodman**, author of *The Babysitter: My Summers with a Serial Killer*

"Conjuring the spirits of Truman Capote and Damon Runyon (with the ghost of Patricia Highsmith looking on), the stories in *The Best New True Crime Stories: Well-Mannered Crooks, Rogues & Criminals* thrillingly depict real-life misdeeds throughout history. An Ecuadorian Robin Hood, an art scandal in Paris, new insights into the life and death of a Depression-era bootlegger—what's not to love?"

—**Abbott Kahler**, *New York Times* bestselling author (as Karen Abbott) of *The Ghosts of Eden Park*

"What a fantastic collection of spellbinding true crime stories from around the world! Each one is deeply researched, thoughtful, and fascinating. This anthology is simply good reading for any fan."

—**Kate Winkler Dawson**, *American Sherlock: Murder, Forensics, and the Birth of American CSI*

"Here be monsters! This brilliant collection of gruesome small-town misdeeds spanning a century and four continents will have you running for the comfort and safety of the big city."

—**Peter Houlahan**, author of *Norco '80*

"This compelling collection of serial killer stories is more than its beautifully told parts—it adds up to a clear and startling portrait of murder as an addiction and the very human demons that haunt the lives of killers and victims alike."

—**Deborah Blum**, author of *The Poisoner's Handbook: Murder and the Birth of Forensic Medicine in Jazz-Age New York*

"An engrossing and multi-faceted anthology for a new era of true crime writing. This fascinating collection goes beyond the procedural to raise important questions about how man's darkest impulses both threaten and consume us—as individuals and as a culture."

—**Piper Weiss**, author of *You All Grow Up and Leave Me*

THE
BEST NEW
TRUE CRIME
STORIES

UNSOLVED CRIMES & MYSTERIES

Also by Mitzi Szereto

The Best New True Crime Stories: Serial Killers

The Best New True Crime Stories: Small Towns

The Best New True Crime Stories: Well-Mannered Crooks, Rogues & Criminals

The Best New True Crime Stories: Crimes of Passion, Obsession & Revenge

The Best New True Crime Stories: Partners in Crime

THE
BEST NEW
TRUE CRIME
STORIES

UNSOLVED CRIMES & MYSTERIES

MITZI SZERETO

mango
PUBLISHING GROUP

CORAL GABLES

Cover Design: & Art Direction Elina Diaz
Cover Photo: fotoru/Adobe Stock
Layout & Design: Katia Mena

For permission requests, please contact the publisher at:
Mango Publishing Group
2850 S Douglas Road, 4th Floor
Coral Gables, FL 33134 USA
info@mango.bz

For special orders, quantity sales, course adoptions and corporate sales, please email the publisher at sales@mango.bz. For trade and wholesale sales, please contact Ingram Publisher Services at customer.service@ingramcontent.com or +1.800.509.4887.

The Best New True Crime Stories: Unsolved Crimes & Mysteries

Library of Congress Cataloging-in-Publication number: 2022939118
ISBN: (print) 978-1-64250-941-0, (ebook) 978-1-64250-942-7
BISAC category code SOC051000, SOCIAL SCIENCE / Violence in Society

Printed in the United States of America

Table of Contents

Introduction

Introduction

*"The impossible cannot have happened, therefore,
the impossible must be possible in spite of appearances."*

—Hercule Poirot via Agatha Christie

There's something appealing about a mystery. Take a "whodunnit," for instance. We enjoy reading them (or watching them) because we know that at the end, we'll find out *who dunnit*. We don't like unanswered questions or being left hanging, even if we enjoy the journey along the way. We like our questions to be answered and all matters relating to those questions resolved. We like the keys to unlock the doors.

But what happens when there aren't any answers or the answers leave you with more questions? Sometimes real-life events can't be wrapped up in a nice tidy package and stored away, particularly when it comes to crime. We want crime cases to be solved. Although we can't necessarily prevent these crimes from happening, at least we can rest a bit easier when we know that the culprits have been caught and brought to justice.

In the United States, the number of unsolved crimes, typically referred to as "cold cases," has been increasing every year. According to FBI data, only 45 percent of violent crimes lead to arrest and prosecution. Crime in the nonviolent category (such as arson, burglary, and car theft) fare even worse at 17 percent. Cold cases are now in a crisis situation, say federal law enforcement officials. And the problem isn't exclusive to the USA. In the United Kingdom, which has a far lower crime rate than America, the number of crimes being solved has reached a new low, while the number of crimes being committed has increased. Lower-crime Canada also has its fair share of unsolved crimes, particularly when it comes to murder. Considering today's advanced forensics techniques, these aren't very reassuring statistics. Rewind to past decades or even past centuries, and it's a wonder anything got solved at all unless the perpetrator was found with the proverbial "smoking gun" in hand.

The Best New True Crime Stories: Unsolved Crimes & Mysteries, the sixth volume in my true crime franchise, explores a variety of crimes that can't be wrapped up in a nice tidy package. You'll find a veritable Rubik's Cube of new and original accounts from many locations and time frames. Some of these accounts have personally touched the lives of those who have written them. From unsolved murders and missing persons cases to daring heists and mysterious deaths, the stories in this anthology will take you on an international true crime journey you won't soon forget.

Mitzi Szereto

Twenty-Five Years Later, This AT Lesbian Double Murder Still Haunts Me

Lindsey Danis

My dream of one day thru-hiking the Appalachian Trail disintegrated in high school when a friend showed me a newspaper clipping. A lesbian couple had been murdered while camping in the backcountry at Shenandoah National Park. Their campsite was half a mile from Skyland Resort, which offers cabin and room rentals, near where the Appalachian Trail cuts through the park.

Julianne (Julie) Williams and Laura (Lollie) Winans weren't hiking the Appalachian Trail when they were killed. They'd taken a camping trip to Shenandoah to celebrate Julie's new job. The couple had recently found a summer home rental in Huntington, Vermont. They'd be able to live together, a welcome change from navigating a long-distance relationship. Instead, Julie's father, Thomas Williams, reported the women missing on May 31, 1996.

Julie was twenty-four when she died. Originally from St. Cloud, Minnesota, she studied geology at Carleton College, graduating summa cum laude. She spoke Spanish and studied abroad in Europe, learning about the extinction of the dinosaurs. She dated men through college and was engaged at one point, but she knew she was attracted to women. After graduation, she worked at a bookstore in laid-back Burlington, Vermont.

She struggled to reconcile her Christian religion with her lesbian identity in an era when an "affirming congregation" was an oxymoron.

Writing for *Out*, Barry Yeoman describes twenty-six-year-old Lollie as a "microbrew-drinking, Phish-following, cigarette-smoking, good-time girl." She fled an upper-class family in Michigan for Vermont, dropping out of college before reenrolling in Maine's Unity College in 1994. Lollie had been sexually abused as a child, and the wilderness helped her heal. She hoped to give other women the same experience and had a dream of becoming a wilderness guide.

———

The two women met in Minnesota's Boundary Waters. They were participants on a trip organized by Woodswomen, a Minneapolis-based nonprofit that specialized in adventure travel for women. "Adventure is the Best Souvenir" ran the organization's tagline, but Lollie and Julie found something more precious in the "Don't Ask Don't Tell" 1990s: each other.

Lollie and Julie arrived in Shenandoah National Park on May 19, along with their golden retriever Taj. At the time, the park's backcountry camping regulations required that campers pitch their tents away from developed areas, including fire roads and trails. Following these guidelines, the pair chose a spot near Bridle Trail, a horse trail that connects Skyland with Big Meadows, a lodge and campground south of Skyland. They camped near a stream. Authorities believe the running water may have masked the sound of approaching feet. I wonder if it hid their screams.

North of Skyland's lodge, park rangers found the women's car. They searched the network of trails that spiral out from Skyland. On one of these searches, they came across Taj, unleashed and wandering. It wasn't until the evening of June 1, the day Julie was due to start her new job, that the women's bodies were found near their campsite.

The lead investigator for the National Park Service, Tim Alley, said that Lollie was found inside the tent with her hands and ankles bound with duct tape. She was gagged. Julie's body was found some thirty to forty feet away, along with her sleeping bag and sleeping pad. Julie's hands were bound, and she was gagged too. They were partially undressed. Their throats were slashed.

In 1996, 1.57 million people visited Shenandoah. Julie and Lollie were killed the week after Memorial Day—prime summer-vacation time. It was hard to believe that a gory double murder could take place minutes from Skyland Resort; Skyline Drive, the scenic byway built by the Civilian Conservation Corps in the 1930s that serves as the park's main road; and the Appalachian Trail, a major hiking destination.

It was hard to believe that no one had heard cries before the women were gagged. That no one spotted an unleashed, wandering dog and thought something was amiss. The women were out of sight, as required by backcountry camping rules. But what about other backcountry campers? Were there really no witnesses, no observers? How had the killer found them, anyway? Had he spied them sharing a kiss on a quiet trail and followed? Or was the incident, which so closely mapped the newly created hate-crime law, actually random? Was it a case of "wrong place, wrong time" for two deeply private women who only felt free to be themselves in the wilderness?

Thru-hikers generally take five to seven months to complete the 2,200-mile trek. Skyland Resort was located some 933 miles from the AT's southern terminus in Georgia. While the earliest of northbound thru-hikers would've passed through the park well before Julie and Lollie's arrival, a steady stream of northbound hikers should've passed through Shenandoah in late May. On the night these women were murdered, thru-hikers would've set up camp just like Julie and Lollie did.

I couldn't stop thinking about the others who might've heard something suspicious and dismissed it as an owl's call. I couldn't stop reviewing the facts of the case, captured with journalistic brevity. Two lesbians were dead in the woods. It could've been random—in fact, that's how the FBI described it—but it sure didn't feel that way to me. I was a closeted baby dyke. I loved the woods and summer camp and the women I met at summer camp, even if I wasn't yet ready to act on those feelings. Julie and Lollie were the same age as my camp counselors. In their smiling faces, and in their grisly murder, I saw my future.

Among the objects discovered at the murder scene was a camera belonging to the women. Film developed after their deaths shows how they spent their time in Shenandoah. First, the two set off on Whiteoak Canyon Trail, a 9.5-mile out and back trail known for its waterfalls and swimming holes. The women returned from the woods a few days later. They caught a ride with a park ranger to renew their backcountry camping permit. They climbed Hawksbill, the highest mountain located inside park boundaries. Finally, they pitched their tent off Bridle Trail, where the killer came across their path.

Neither Julie nor Lollie had come out to their families. The two were outed by Rebecca Strader, minister at the Burlington, Vermont, church Julie attended, who decided it was in the best interest of the LGBTQ community to be honest about their relationship, even if the women were discreet. Their relatives learned of the women's sexuality and their relationship through the subsequent media blitz.

LGBTQ people processed the news the same way I did: with shock, fear, and anxiety. Activists made sure the case grabbed headlines. Many felt certain the women had been targeted for their sexuality, and that their lesbian identities could be critical to catching the killer. Others wanted to make sure Julie and Lollie weren't erased in death as they'd been silenced in life: by a homophobic culture, and then, quite literally, by their killer.

There aren't a lot of crimes that happen on park lands. Most people who want to experience nature tend to tread lightly in the wilderness, after all. When something does go wrong, the investigation is more complex than with other murders.

First, there's jurisdiction, or investigating authority. Shenandoah's jurisdiction is federal, which leaves the federal government with sole duty as law enforcement. FBI officials descended on the site, as did a crime scene unit from the Virginia State Police. "At the time we did not have the equipment [to] process the crime scene," recalled Bridget Bohnet, Deputy Chief Ranger at Shenandoah National Park at the time. With three investigating authorities on site, only one of which—the FBI—had jurisdiction, the investigation soon got bogged down with procedural infighting.

Then there's the crime scene itself, which is likely to sprawl over remote, potentially inaccessible terrain. The Bridle Trail campsite connected to a large radius of park lands, with multiple trailheads and access points on which to hunt for clues. "Any type of crime that occurs in an outdoor environment, your crime scene is probably ten times larger than it would be in a residence. You have the initial crime scene where something happened, and then you have the outer crime scene, because you don't know which way the person came in or went. So the crime scene in and of itself tends to be larger and harder to contain and process," Bohnet explained.

Although the Park Service found the women's bodies shortly after their investigation began, they didn't release the news publicly for thirty-six hours. This gave the killer ample time to leave the area relatively unobserved. When he announced the murder, acting Park Superintendent Greg Stiles downplayed it as an "isolated" incident, despite there being no evidence that it was.

The authorities pursued some fifteen thousand leads. Williams's former fiancé was asked to take a polygraph, as were several park employees. The FBI tested fingerprints and hair samples from several park employees. They put out a $25,000 reward. They looked for connections with other cases, most notably an unsolved 1986 lesbian double murder that took place near Williamsburg, Virginia. There, two women were discovered with bound wrists, rope burns, and slashed throats in a car pushed off an embankment near a popular gay cruising spot. Thirteen months later, a second incident off Skyline Drive would hand the authorities the suspect they'd been searching for.

In July 1997, a man in a truck forced a Canadian female cyclist off her bike along Skyline Drive. The driver yelled sexually aggressive things like "Show me your titties!" while he tried to force the cyclist, Yvonne Malbasha, into his truck. Malbasha was able to escape his grasp by using her bicycle as a wedge between them. She took shelter behind a tree. The guy got back in his truck and gunned it toward her, attempting to run her down before he gave up and fled the scene. "The vehicle came so close, I could actually feel the heat of the engine," she said afterward.

Fortunately for Malbasha, the first car to pass by was a park ranger who carried a cell phone. He sent out a description of the assailant. Park rangers were able to stop him before he could leave the park. A search of his truck turned up leg and hand restraints similar to those used on Julie and Lollie. After Malbasha identified the man, he was taken into custody.

Darrell David Rice, Malbasha's attacker, was a single, childless twenty-something living in Columbia, Maryland (incidentally, the place where I was born). A Charlottesville, Virginia, newspaper, *The Hook*, reported that Rice had been fired from his job the previous month due to extreme hostility at work. His former coworkers reported several disturbing behaviors. Rice frequently yelled profanities, including sexual slurs. He bumped into female coworkers, causing them to spill hot coffee. He punched a hole in the men's bathroom wall. He took down a female colleague's photo and threw it in the trash.

Statements Rice made during interviews after his arrest gave prosecutors reason to believe he might have killed Julie and Lollie. All of his intended victims were female; the majority of his hostile work behavior was directed toward women. It was the same location, the same choice of restraints, and the same predatory behavior.

Rice pled guilty to the attempted abduction of Malbasha in 1998 and received a sentence of 135 months (or eleven years) in a federal penitentiary. Meanwhile, the authorities continued to build their case for the Shenandoah murders.

The FBI sent an undercover agent to speak with Rice during his imprisonment. Rice told the agent that he had only previous sexual relationships with women, most recently in 1991. He complained of sexual inadequacy and an inability to get a girlfriend.

These words bear strong similarity to remarks made by "incels," or involuntarily celibate men. Unable to find girlfriends, incels treat women with violence and hostility. To date, forty to fifty women in the US and Canada have been murdered by men with some allegiance to the incel mindset, Alex DiBranco, the executive director at the Institute for Research on Male Supremacism, and Jacob Ware, a terrorism researcher who studies the incel movement, told *The Guardian*. Men feel entitled to female romantic attention. If they don't get what they believe they deserve, women can be killed for it.

Rice had a motive: he wanted attention from women and was unsuccessful in romance. He also had an opportunity. Video footage showed Rice entering Shenandoah National Park on May 25, 1996, at the northern entrance in Front Royal; on May 26, 1996, at Rockfish Gap; and a third time, in the company of two friends, on June 1, 1996. Rice denied his first two visits, but did admit to being there on June 1.

As a result of this circumstantial evidence, Attorney General John Ashcroft charged Rice with Julie and Lollie's murder on April 10, 2001. The indictment focused on Rice's misogyny, as evidenced in his attack on Malbasha, his behavior toward his former coworkers, and his comments about women's physical vulnerability as opposed to men's. Rice was quoted as saying that Julie and Lollie "deserved to die because they were lesbian whores."

Rice was charged with four counts of capital murder. Two of these were hate crime charges, among the first to be filed after a 1994 law that permitted elevated charges on bias crimes. If convicted of a hate crime, Rice could be sentenced to death.

Before Rice could be prosecuted, however, new evidence led to the dismissal of charges.

Initially, prosecutors tested mitochondrial DNA from the women's clothing. This type of DNA determined the sex of the killer, but nothing more significant emerged. In October 2003, a hair obtained from the tape on Lollie's wrists was tested using a new DNA test, Y-STR. This test indicated that the DNA found at the scene did not belong to Rice. With the new discovery, the case fell apart.

The prosecution had charged Rice based on largely circumstantial evidence. Without DNA evidence, the case was not viable. The defense claimed prosecutorial misconduct, pointing to several problems with the prosecution's case. The defense alleged that investigators, under pressure to solve a murder, tried to manipulate witnesses, including a couple that had camped in Shenandoah on the night of the murder.

The homophobic comment mentioned in Rice's indictment was incorrectly transcribed to appear more inflammatory than it actually was, the defense suggested. While Rice struggled with drug abuse and depression, relatives believed he was getting his life together at the time of the murder. They painted a picture of a hippie-ish Grateful Dead fan who had close female and gay friends. Those close to Rice agreed that he was troubled, but couldn't see him as violent or homophobic.

In 2004, the charges were dismissed without prejudice, leaving the door open to charge Rice in the future should new evidence turn up. Rice served ten years in prison for the assault on Malbasha. He was released in 2007, but returned to prison over parole violations in 2009, then again in 2010.

Twenty-five years after Julie and Lollie were murdered, the FBI is still actively investigating the crime. For the milestone anniversary in 2021, the FBI updated their Seeking Information posters with additional photos of the women. A press release written by Public Affairs Specialist Dennette (Dee) Rybiski reads: "The beauty of Virginia's Parks and Trails are enticing to people, not just from Virginia, but other states;

and during these outdoor adventures people come across other hikers and visitors—some who make a memorable impression. Over the past twenty-five years we are cognizant that those who were hiking in the park at the time of the murders, were visiting local establishments, and even resided in the area may not be local to Virginia any longer—therefore it is crucial that this case continues to be shared throughout the country. It is possible there are people anywhere from Virginia to the west coast that could have information valuable to investigators."

In an opinion published in *The Washington Post* in June 2021, Deirdre M. Enright, the founder and director of the Innocence Project at the University of Virginia School of Law, calls this continued investigation "futile," saying that "it overlooks the obvious forensic avenues that could solve this case." Enright was part of Rice's defense team for the Shenandoah murders and subsequent charges. She believes the DNA tests prove conclusively that Rice did not kill Julie and Lollie. Instead, she maintains, they point the finger at confirmed serial killer Richard Evonitz.

Evonitz was a Navy man, a seemingly nice guy who preyed on teenage girls. In 2002, after a fifteen-year-old girl he abducted and raped escaped from the apartment where he was holding her and went to the police, Evonitz fled. While on the run, he confessed to the abduction and murder of three girls, ages twelve to sixteen. Evonitz told his sister he had committed more crimes than he could remember before he shot himself rather than be taken in by police.

After his death, authorities took DNA samples. Subsequent lab testing linked him to the murders of three teens in 1996 and 1997. Two of his victims had been sexually assaulted, with their pubic hair shaved. The FBI promised to evaluate Evonitz against other unsolved murders, both in Virginia and across the nation. Reporting by *The Free Lance-Star* indicated that subsequent testing was incomplete as of 2007, despite a supervisor's recommendation to check Evonitz against DNA gathered from the Shenandoah crime scene and another local case.

In 1996, Evonitz had lived in Spotsylvania, Virginia. Skyland Resort was less than two hours away. Records indicate that Evonitz called off work on May 30 and May 31, 1996. Like Rice, he had both opportunity and a history of violence against women.

The same DNA test that ruled out Rice revealed Evonitz as a potential match. The hair from Lollie's bindings matched 8 percent of the US population, a sample group that included Evonitz. The FBI ordered no further forensic testing to determine whether Evonitz could be their suspect.

"As anniversaries of the crimes come and go, the government has staunchly refused to test the DNA for a link to Evonitz and to pursue the very real possibility that they already have the evidence needed to solve this case. DNA tests showed that hairs found in gloves at the crime scene and in the duct tape used to bind the victims were from the same source and matched Evonitz's hairs at all but two of 650 base pairs on a mitochondrial chain. In 2004, the government called that 'inconclusive.' Several labs have assured us that there are now tests available that would likely produce conclusive results. There is male DNA on one of the gags, and it isn't Rice's. There are lubricants in both victims, and they cannot be linked to either victim or Rice. Evonitz had many lubricants," Enright writes.

Enright calls on the FBI to pursue the Evonitz lead rather than engage in showmanship. Despite urging from their family members to do so, authorities have yet to fully test the DNA evidence that could provide firm answers and closure for Julie and Lollie's loved ones.

Rice may be a free man after serving time for his assault on Malbasha, but the Shenandoah murders still have him in their grip. They've got me too. Lesbians and AT thru-hikers have been murdered in the years since Julie and Lollie's deaths, but I don't know their names.

Julie and Lollie's murders brought brutality to public lands, places that Americans are taught to believe belong to them. As a child, I felt safe to explore the woods. By imprinting the lesson that gay women were unsafe outdoors, Julie and Lollie's murders taught me to fear the wilderness. Their deaths shattered my innocence, though I'd have scoffed at the use of that word.

I visited Shenandoah National Park in 2016, on the twentieth anniversary of the case. It was late June, my mother's birthday. The two of us parked at Skyland Resort and hiked to Little Stony Man. It was a relatively easy hike, forested terrain giving way to a mild rock scramble that offered sweeping views. In the photos we took at the top, I posed with the mountains at my back and a smile on my face. Julie and Lollie were on my mind, but I wasn't going to bring it up in front of my mother. She worried enough about my safety as it was.

Hiking down the mountain, we came to a trail juncture. While we paused to consult our map, a man emerged from the woods. Two golden retrievers followed at his heels. "You should see this, it's really cool," he told us, pointing down a side trail. I thought of Julie and Lollie, and of Taj, their golden retriever. I wondered how far we stood from where they'd set up camp. It must've looked like this, I imagined: a network of trails, where a wide fire road met the narrow dirt path of the horse trail, where, if the insects quieted, you might hear a babbling brook.

If Julie and Lollie had gone down a different path, I thought, then shook my head. The women had made countless small decisions during their time in the park: which trail to hike, where to break for lunch or take a dip in a cold mountain stream, where to sleep for the night, when to chance a hug or a kiss, something they felt safe doing in the privacy of the woods. I made the same calculations when I hiked the Hudson Valley, where I lived.

I would never know if their killer had observed some display of affection between the two women. If he'd interrupted them in an intimate act, or if he'd guessed at the nature of their relationship, or if one had tried to protect the other by bargaining with the killer. I would never know these things, unless there was a new development in the case. That was the problem with being a queer traveler: you would never know where the line between safe and unsafe lay until you crossed it, and by then it was too late.

We followed the stranger. I pushed down my misgivings: it was daylight, there was nothing to fear. He led us to the pump house for Furnace Springs, where a wooden door with rusted latches was built into a rocky outcropping. With moss and ferns growing amid the rocks, it looked like a hobbit house. We thanked him for showing us, then walked the last leg of the trail.

On the balcony at Skyland, sharing a post-hike snack, I relaxed. The stranger had been excited about an unusual find and wanted to show someone. I'd let history get the better of me. I'd visited several national parks with my mother previously, and I'd never felt unsafe. I didn't feel unsafe in Shenandoah, not exactly, but the grisly double murder cast a shadow over my visit.

I returned to Shenandoah in 2021, for the twenty-fifth anniversary of Julie and Lollie's murders. The park offered a convenient halfway place to break up a long drive. I was still thinking about the case, turning it over in my mind as if I could unravel the strands of fear and find a home in the woods once more. This time, my wife and I camped inside the park.

It was after midnight, well past the campground's quiet hours. People had been arriving all night. Most set up quietly, mindful of the late hours. A nearby group played music, laughed, and screamed. I tried to ignore the loud group, but every time I felt myself drifting toward sleep, their noise cut through the night. We took a walk, figuring we'd politely ask them to be quiet. "You better keep walking!" yelled a long-haired guy at the offending site. A woman hung on an open truck door, laughing loudly. Others stood and watched us. I felt their eyes on me as we walked toward the bathroom—the one plausible destination for a late-night walk—and past it. I felt the target on my back, the same one that kept me off the AT.

While passing their site earlier, I'd been hit with something. I brushed it off, thinking a tween had accidentally shot a Nerf gun toward the road. My neck prickled as I realized it had been no accident. Like Rice bumping into his female coworkers so they spilled coffee, the aggressive camper had been testing the limits. While there were plenty of people around to bear witness, my gut told me to keep walking.

We continued around the loop road until we found the campground host. He was an older man, retired and RVing while earning part-time income hosting for the campsite. When we explained the situation, he sighed and said he'd take care of it. "No worries, that's what I'm here for," he said after we apologized for waking him.

On the walk back to our site, we decided to break down camp. We'd stuff our tent, clothing, camp chairs, and gear into our hatchback, changing sites to avoid retaliation. I had a bad feeling about that group, and I wasn't leaving myself vulnerable. As we approached our site, I could hear the host talking to the loud campers. Soon, someone roared off in a truck modified with loud exhaust pipes. We resettled, but I was too keyed-up for sleep.

In the morning, the camp host drove by our new location. He told me the group was probably high, that he'd smelled marijuana. If they hadn't quieted down, he would've called the authorities. While he was out, he'd also shut down another loud campsite. "It's a shame some people have to ruin it for the rest of us," I told him. I wanted to say more. On its face, this was as much a random, isolated incident as Julie and Lollie's murders had been. But of course, it wasn't either of those things. It fit the long-established, identifiable pattern of male violence toward women.

An hour later, we left the campsite and headed for Hawksbill, one of the last hikes Julie and Lollie took. The trail was wide, rocky, and dark, shaded by a forest canopy that blocked most of the late June heat and humidity. We passed groups of hikers: a mother with two teenage boys, a father with three adult children and an illegally off-leash poodle mix, and two older couples. The women blazed uphill while their husbands lagged behind, leaning on hiking poles. I joked to my wife that I hoped we'd be like those women when we were older.

The trees thinned out. A signpost came into view. We were nearly there. To our right was Byrd's Nest, a stone day-use shelter. The summit was fifty feet away, with a viewing platform. Groups stood on rocky outcroppings, taking in views of the distant valley. A town was hazy in the distance. This was my country, but I would never feel at home in it—for me, that's the lasting legacy of the Shenandoah National Park murders.

The Great Montréal Museum Heist Of 1972

Anya Wassenberg

A spectacular entry into a stately museum, a trio of obviously educated and athletic thieves, and millions of dollars in artwork and jewelry that remain missing and unrecovered nearly a half-century later—it's a scenario that could have been lifted from the script of the latest Hollywood criminal-caper flick.

In the dark of night on September 4, 1972, three men broke into the Montréal Museum of Fine Arts in Montréal, Canada, through a skylight in the roof. It was a little past midnight, and it was the Labor Day long weekend, which meant most of the museum's administrators, including the head of security, the president, and director, were on vacation.

The MMFA's collection was packed with masterworks of Western art and had been assembled from the private collections and donations of many of Canada's wealthiest families over its then 112-year history. Moreover, the museum's collection of high-profile artworks was fairly well known not only regionally but across North America, because of an exhibition that had toured through the United States during the months leading up to the Montréal Expo in 1967.

After the shocking theft, for several years, the story of the investigation and aftermath unfolded largely behind the scenes and out of the public eye as hope for a break in the case persisted. While the case files are technically closed, the Montréal police department and other law enforcement agencies involved have not released any of their contents.

Details of the robbery and investigations come from newspaper accounts and interviews published over the years, including several articles in the *Montreal Gazette*, the city's daily English-language newspaper, and the work of a couple of people who've made the unsolved crime a professional passion.

Alain Lacoursière was a twenty-five-year veteran of the police force. He became a specialist in art crime investigation after becoming a fraud detective in 1994. With a passion for art history and plenty of contacts in the art world, he made the museum heist one of his pet projects, giving many print and broadcast interviews on the subject.

Art historian Catherine Schofield Sezgin is editor of the blog for the Association of Research into Crimes against Art (ARCA). Sezgin wrote an extensive paper on the heist published in the *Journal of Art Crime*. Published by the ARCA, the academic journal has an international editorial masthead and a board of trustees with members including Dennis Ahearn, Director of Security at Christie's in London, and other experts.

Lacoursière and Sezgin often collaborated in keeping the details of the massive art theft alive through interviews and stories, even as the police trail grew cold.

A Daring Yet Meticulous Crime

From the details of the crime, it becomes clear that the thieves were meticulous and athletic and had planned the heist down to nearly the last detail.

The museum itself, designed in a decorative Beaux-Arts style, had been constructed in 1912, with few, if any, major upgrades since that period. The MMFA's exhibition of paintings was housed in a three-story structure, at the time about sixty years old. It stands squarely on Sherbrooke Street, one of Montréal's main throughfares.

The first thief had picks on his boots, similar to the kind used by telecom workers to scale telephone and hydropower poles. Using the picks, he scuttled his way up a tree conveniently located next to the museum's main building, about twenty feet above the ground. From there, he jumped onto the roof. At the time, the museum was undergoing some exterior renovations. After making his way to the roof, the thief lowered a ladder that had been left by workers who were repairing the roofing, and the two other robbers followed him up.

The construction crew had left a loosely tied plastic sheet over the museum's open skylight, which would, under normal circumstances, have been connected to the building's main security system. With the alarm taken out of the equation, the thieves were able to slip inside the building unnoticed from above by shimmying down a nylon cord.

As they dropped to the floor, the trio quickly encountered a security guard. One of the three museum guards on duty was on his break and alone when he first encountered the robbers. The thieves ordered him onto the ground, and when he didn't immediately do as he was told, one of them fired two shots into the ceiling with a 12-gauge pump shotgun. The first guard was subdued after the show of intimidation and tied up. The other two guards came running after hearing the shotgun blast, but the trio of thieves took them by surprise, and they were tied up alongside the first.

In later interviews, the guards mentioned seeing two long-haired men (not an uncommon sight in Montréal in 1972) wearing masks. They only heard the voice of the third. All three thieves wore ski masks and hoods, and from the guards' testimony, two were French-speaking while a third spoke English, an important distinction in the city, which was fraught with francophone-driven separatism at the time.

After the initial commotion, one of the thieves held the guards at gunpoint while the other two set about the work of gathering the paintings by cutting them out of their frames.

The total haul that made it out of the building in their clutches included eighteen paintings and thirty-nine pieces of jewelry, valued then at two million Canadian dollars. The big prize among the stolen canvases was a Rembrandt titled *Landscape with Cottages*, an oil-on-panel painting dated 1654 and attributed to the Dutch master. It alone was valued at one million dollars, and today is estimated to be worth as much as fifty million. Other stolen works included pieces by Eugène Delacroix, Pieter Brueghel the Elder, Thomas Gainsborough, Jean-Baptiste-Camille Corot, Gustave Courbet, Honoré Daumier, Jean-François Millet, Peter Paul Rubens, and two portraits by François-André Vincent.

The items of jewelry included a gold watch from France, made in the eighteenth century, that had belonged to the wife of Montréal's first elected mayor, Jacques Viger.

But the thieves' ambitions were apparently even greater. Along with shards of glass from smashed cases and broken picture frames worth a small fortune on their own, the thieves had abandoned canvases by El Greco, Tintoretto, Picasso, and even another Rembrandt, all of which were left sitting on the floor ready for transport. In total, they had already taken another fifteen paintings from the walls, with the obvious intention of making off with them too.

As it happened, they'd run into their first, and perhaps *only*, bit of bad luck—a snag that would throw complications in the way of their carefully planned heist.

With their first haul settled upon, the plan, ostensibly, was to load up what they'd already bagged up and come back for the rest. The trio first attempted to exit the building via a system of pulleys that would have carried them back up to the skylight to then clamber out again over the roof and down the ladder. However, that process seemed to be taking too long, and the pulleys were abandoned. Taking a set of keys from one of the guards, the art thieves attempted to leave the building by a side door via stairs down to a garage, and then load up one of the museum's panel trucks with their loot.

However, while carrying out the first load of art and jewelry, one of the masked robbers tripped an alarm at the side entrance. Once they heard it, the remaining canvases were abandoned, and the thieves grabbed the rolled-up paintings, stuffed jewels into their pockets, and took off down the street with whatever they could carry.

What the trio of daring thieves didn't realize was that the alarm at the side door wasn't connected to anything outside the museum building; it would only have notified the guards who were already tied up. Luckily for the museum, the ambitious robbers thought police were already on the way, and they fled on foot down the darkened street.

All in all, the thieves were in and out of the museum in about thirty minutes.

It took another hour, but one of the guards finally managed to free himself. In accordance with museum protocol, he informed the police as well as the museum's director of public relations, Bill Bantey. Bantey had been a journalist before taking on the role of PR director.

In a broadcast on CBC Radio at the time, Bantey commented, "It would seem that they were discriminating thieves and had a fairly good idea of what they were looking for, certainly in terms of pictures…in terms of jewelry, it's open to debate."

Ruth Jackson, curator of decorative arts, was also one of the first museum employees to arrive on the scene. She got there not long after the police and began the work of surveying and cataloguing the damage. The scope of the theft was breathtaking. Jackson told the *Montreal Gazette* later in an interview, "With what they'd proposed to remove, it was just like they meant a general clear-out of the museum."

The Investigation

For months, there was essentially a news blackout as the police searched for leads. Interpol had been notified, and all the border crossings along the Canadian-American border were on alert. But other than broken glass and frames in splinters, the thieves left very little for police to go on. There were no fingerprints left at the scene, and the shotguns used during the robbery were never recovered.

It was thought that the city's unique political and social culture could have played a role in the stunning theft in more ways than one.

Montréal in the late 1960s and early 1970s was a city of vibrant culture and arts fueled by its dual French and English roots and bolstered by Canada's policy of multiculturalism and immigration reform. It was still coming off the high of international exposure that the 1967 International and Universal Exposition, or Expo 67, as it was more commonly called, had brought to the city.

As part of Expo 67, the museum's most impressive paintings toured major galleries in the United States from January 1966 to April 1967, taking them from Florida to Ohio and New York in an exhibition called *Masterpieces from Montréal: Selected Paintings from the Collection of the Montréal Museum of Fine Arts.* Half of the paintings that were stolen had been spotlighted in the traveling show's catalogue. They included de Heem's *Nature Morte*, Corot's *La Rêveuse à la Fontaine*, Courbet's *Landscape with Rocks and Streams*, Delacroix's *Lioness and Lion in a Cave*, Diaz de la Peña's *The Sorceress*, Thomas Gainsborough's *Portrait of Brigadier General Sir Thomas Fletcher*, de Heem's *Nature Morte au Poisson*, and Piazzetta's *Portrait of a Man*.

Bilingual Montréal, the business and arts capital of the province, was also a flash point for tensions between French- and English-speaking factions, including groups that advocated for separation of the province of Québec from Canada. In 1970, just two years before the robbery, those tensions had boiled over into a series of events called the "October Crisis," involving separatist terrorists and the kidnapping and murder of British and provincial cabinet minister Pierre Laporte. The army had been called in by Prime Minister Pierre Trudeau to quell the separatist unrest, but the political climate was still volatile.

There was a long-standing history of friction between the French-speaking students of l'École des Beaux-Arts de Montréal (Montréal School of Fine Arts) and the English-speaking museum and its administrators that had been the subject of public commentary for years. At first, suspicions fell on a group of students at the art school.

The crime certainly pointed to parties with a knowledge of art and the museum's collection. According to Alain Lacoursière, as quoted in the *Journal of Art Crime*, "For fifteen days, the police followed five suspects, night and day." With no results that could point to the heist, however, the tail was dropped.

The ladder and the nylon ropes yielded no forensic leads. Because of the rather spectacular and athletic means of entry, police suspected they were up against an international gang of some kind. There were Italian, Irish, and French-Canadian gangsters active in the city, along with criminal biker gangs, leaving a large pool of potential parties of interest.

Intriguingly, an art theft with similar outlines—a risky and physically difficult entry, and a highly targeted haul of paintings—had taken place a few days before in a community about twenty miles west of Montréal. On August 30, three armed men wearing hoods broke into the home of Agnes Meldrum in Oka, Québec, and made off with about fifty thousand dollars' worth of paintings from her private collection. It was the summer home of a woman who owned a large moving company in Montréal with her husband. To gain entry to her property, the thieves had taken a motorboat out on the Lake of Two Mountains, then climbed up a steep six-hundred-foot bluff. In that investigation, the police believed locals were responsible, probably because of their familiarity with the landscape. The investigation yielded few clues.

An article published in the *Montreal Gazette* in December 1972 quoted unnamed sources who claimed that some of the stolen paintings had been transported to the US, while the rest had been divided between wealthy denizens of Montréal's tony Ville de Mont-Royal neighborhood. After following the trail, police questioned two suspects, but no leads emerged.

Naturally, the investigation took police inside to the museum's employees, but this too, led to a dead end. "No one on the museum staff was involved," Bantey said in a 2010 interview. "If there was any inside information, it probably emanated from the people working on the skylight repairs."

The workers who had been doing the roof repairs came under intense scrutiny and questioning. Some witnesses said they saw two men sitting on the roof of the building a couple of weeks before the heist. The men wore sunglasses and were sitting on chairs and claimed to be working at the museum when questioned. Later, when the roof was searched thoroughly, their chairs were missing.

However, one point of significance was that, while the thieves knew about the work on the roof and the skylight alarm system, they acted in a way that made clear their ignorance of how any of the other alarms operated (as evidenced by the way they'd tripped the door alarm). That tended to rule out an inside job when it came to the renovation workers or the museum's employees, pointing instead to clever and resourceful outsiders who'd done their homework as far as they'd been able to.

In 1972, if an auction house did not manually check the Interpol database of stolen works—which even the major auctioneers didn't do before the 1980s—it's possible the paintings were quickly sold to owners who believed they were legitimately provenanced, if the sale took place almost immediately after they'd been stolen. It was a long shot, but authorities had to consider all the possibilities.

Ransom Attempts

Stealing valuable paintings and holding them for ransom is fairly common in the upper echelons of art theft. Selling such works is often out of the question unless the buyer is already in on the theft, since the notoriety of stolen pieces precludes public auctions or any above-board sale. Various criminal factions that were active in the city were also known to deal in the black market for stolen artworks, including the Hell's Angels and the Italian Mafia.

Not long after the heist, David Giles Carter, who served as director of the museum at the time, was contacted by one of the thieves by phone, looking to negotiate a return of the works for ransom. Carter asked for the return of one or two pieces as a show of good faith. The caller told the museum to send someone to a specific phone booth. Once there, the museum employee got another call with instructions to look for a cigarette package on the ground. The museum staff member found one of the stolen pendants inside the discarded pack.

Carter would later dub the thief "Port of Montréal." After the pendant was recovered, Carter received a brown Port of Montréal envelope, purportedly from the thieves, which contained photographs of the stolen paintings. Along with the snaps came their final demand: they wanted $500,000 in cash. That figure, based on an evaluation of 25 percent of the paintings' worth, was later dropped to $250,000 during the ongoing negotiations.

A museum security guard, acting under the thieves' instructions, went to a locker at Montréal's central train station. There he found one of the stolen Brueghel paintings.

After another communication from the thieves, a Montréal cop posing as an insurance adjuster was told to wait in a vacant field just outside the city with five thousand dollars in cash that was to be exchanged for one of the paintings. Unaware of the undercover drop-off that was taking place, an unsuspecting local cop in a police cruiser drove by the site to check it out, and the thieves took it as a sign of police involvement. Disappointingly, no one showed to pick up the money. The next day, an angry voice on the phone would tell Carter that they'd spotted the police surveillance, and communications were cut off.

Alain Lacoursière's November 2009 interview on the subject is quoted in the *Journal of Art Crime*. "It could have all been a smokescreen," he said. "The meeting was set up in a field with no houses around. The thieves could have seen the cops moving into the set-up. In 1972, few cars would have been passing by, and it would have been easy to spot four to five cop cars. They never tried again, so it was a smokescreen. Look, when the museum first asked for proof that the thieves had the paintings, the one painting that was returned was a fake."

A fake? As it turns out, there was yet another twist in the story, when it came to the Brueghel piece titled *Landscape with Buildings and Wagon* that was stolen and later returned. Since the wooden frame had been irreparably damaged during the robbery, the painting sat in a storage facility for about a decade after its recovery until another frame suitable for a masterpiece could be fitted for it. During that period, though, the authenticity of the work was challenged. After a review by the museum and experts in the field, the canvas was eventually ascribed to the School of Jan Brueghel the Elder, not to the master himself. That's how it was eventually listed after it was reframed and displayed once more on the museum's walls in the early 1980s.

In May 1973, the museum was shuttered for three years for a major renovation and overhaul of its systems. That summer, another member of the board of directors got an anonymous call. This time, the caller promised to reveal the location of the paintings in exchange for ten thousand dollars. An insurance adjuster got involved in the transaction, and while the museum ponied up the cash, the adjuster made the deal.

According to a 1982 article in the *Gazette*, the adjuster was sent on a wild ride through the city—first to a phone booth in the downtown area, then to a racetrack, and then more phone booths throughout Montréal. During a call at a phone booth near a subway station, the mystery caller claimed to have spotted the police tail. The insurance adjuster assured the supposed thief that he'd get the cops to back down, which he did.

Another call to the phone booth thirty minutes later told the adjuster to return to his office. When he did, the supposed thieves called again, and another round of phone booths ensued, continuing until four in the morning. Finally, the adjuster was told to leave the bag with the cash in front of a sign in another vacant lot. After dropping off the money, he returned to the phone booth, where the thieves were to call again and tell him where the paintings were hidden.

However, the phone booth remained silent. At about eight in the morning, the adjuster got a call at his office. He was instructed to look for the paintings in a motel just outside the city. Police showed up en masse to do a thorough search, but nothing was found on the scene, leading to another dead end in the case and another ten thousand dollars gone.

While it seems clear that the first contact was made by the real robbers, it's not certain whether the second round of calls came from the same group or someone simply wanting to cash in on the notorious heist.

According to Lacoursière, the thieves were consummate pros who set up the bungled ransom attempts and elaborate drop-offs to keep police focused elsewhere while the paintings were whisked out of the country. Customs and border authorities had been informed as well as Interpol. But in 1972, manual methods of getting the word out weren't as simple, and certainly not instantaneous, as the internet makes them now.

After the second ransom attempt, the trail went cold. Despite the fact that the details of the case scream inside job, the police were not able to identify any suspects among the museum's employees or contractors. Insurance investigators who took over also failed to turn up any solid leads.

With international events like the massacre of Israeli athletes by the PLO (Palestine Liberation Organization) at the Munich Olympics quickly taking over the news cycle, the story, along with any leads, quickly died down. Yet the case remained of interest to many people, especially Alain Lacoursière. Decades later, in 1999, on behalf of the police force, Lacoursière offered one million dollars for information about the paintings, though nothing came of it.

In a television documentary from Radio-Canada in 2007 called *Le Colombo de l'Art* (*The Columbo of Art*, a reference to the famous TV detective played by Peter Falk), Lacoursière publicly confronted one of the former art school students who had been tailed back in 1972. On the show, Lacoursière claimed the person in question had proved he had knowledge of very specific details that only the thieves themselves would be aware of—like the type of nylon rope used in the robbery—along with what he characterized as suspicious finances, the student having apparently come into a significant sum of money a short time after the heist.

On camera, Lacoursière offered the man cash for a chance to search his home for the paintings. The man laughed and invited the crew into his home, where no paintings were found. It made for good TV, but did not aid in the investigation.

In 1972, the museum's entire collection had been insured to the tune of eight million dollars. A reward of fifty thousand dollars was posted by the insurance company for any information leading to arrests or the recovery of the art and jewelry. When the police leads dried up and the phone calls stopped coming, the claim was eventually paid to the tune of just under two million, with the risk spread over twenty insurance companies, including Marine Office of America.

While technically it's Lloyd's that would now own the paintings, if recovered, the MMFA would get first dibs on repurchasing them.

Coda

Neither of the ransom attempts was published in the newspapers when they occurred, though the files were still open and the investigation still very much alive. It took a decade before that part of the story was told publicly. At about the same time, the police and insurance files were officially closed.

In the world of fine art heists, unsolved robberies are not so rare. With the insurance claims paid, there's little urgency about the half-century-old crime. But some will never forget, including the former MMFA administrators who were left dealing with the aftermath and a significant fine art collection that had been gutted.

"Everyone forgot about the theft except for the insurance companies," Bill Bantey said in a 2009 interview. "Like a death in the family, you have to let it drop."

Still, theories linger.

"There's a theory that they [the paintings] are in South America," Bantey continued. "Don't ask me to justify it. I've heard several people I respect say that."

According to a 2007 follow-up article in the *Gazette*, David Giles Carter notes that the paintings may have become too notorious to be put on the black market for art, and may, in a worst-case scenario, even have been destroyed.

In the same article, Sean B. Murphy, who was the museum's president at the time, theorizes that it may have been a "robbery on consignment," with the works destined for a private collection in South America. "Many wonderful things happened at the museum during my presidency," Murphy noted, "but this was the worst. The lessons of the robbery are that a museum needs a first-rate security system and the insurance to go with it."

The Montréal Museum of Fine Arts's current security system is said to be state-of-the-art. The 1972 heist remains the largest unsolved art theft in Canadian history.

The Lady Vanishes: The Mysterious Disappearance of Jean Spangler

Joan Renner

The Black Dahlia

At ten in the morning on January 15, 1947, Los Angeles police receive an anonymous telephone call from a woman on the verge of hysteria. In short, emotional bursts, she tells them she found a woman lying in a vacant lot on Norton Avenue, near 39th Street, in Leimert Park. The police want to know if the woman is drunk or in distress. The caller hangs up.

Police half-expect to find an inebriated woman in the weeds of the vacant lot. Instead, they discover the mutilated, naked body of a young woman. The body lies one foot from the sidewalk, and fifty feet north of a fire hydrant. Drained of blood and cut in half at the waist, the corpse is obscenely posed with its legs wide apart and its arms bent above the head. The killer places the body's head to the north, feet to the south. The Hollywood sign is visible on a hillside ten miles away.

There is no identification. No handbag and no clothing. The vacant lot is a body dump site, not a murder scene.

Two days later, police identify the deceased as twenty-two-year-old Elizabeth Short. Short is a small-town girl from Medford, Massachusetts, one of thousands of young women and men adrift in post-war Los Angeles.

Despite countless man-hours spent searching for a crime scene and a killer, by October 1949, the case remains unsolved.

Postwar Los Angeles is unsafe for women. Hundreds of returning veterans suffer serious emotional trauma. They turn to alcohol, drugs, and violence as a balm for their pain and their rage.

Incidents of spousal and child abuse increase, as do reports of rape, murder, and disappearances of women. The perpetrators of the violence against women are not only military personnel. They are transients. Loners and losers. They are predators who instinctively understand that Los Angeles is perfect for hunting human prey.

In early September 1949, the Los Angeles grand jury announces its intention to launch a full-scale investigation into police failure to solve nine recent Black Dahlia-type mutilation murders. The jury foreman, Harry Lawson, chides the LAPD, saying, "There is every possibility that we will summon officers involved in the investigation of these murders. We find it odd that there are on the books of the Los Angeles Police Department so many unsolved crimes of this type."

What the grand jury cannot appreciate is how difficult it is to solve stranger murders. When no relationship exists between the killer and victim, the suspect pool is infinite. In other homicides, all police have to do is confront a spouse or lover, and chances are good they have the killer. In the Black Dahlia case, hundreds of officers door-knock at residences and businesses searching for a crime scene they never find.

As awful as the murders are, the mysterious disappearances of several local women are worse for their families. Unlike the families of the murder victims, the survivors, kept on tenterhooks, cannot mourn the missing in the same way they could the dead.

Hollywood Dreams

During the 1940s, as they have for nearly three decades, young women ignore the dangers and flock to the city seeking fame and fortune. Greyhound buses drop off dozens of Hollywood hopefuls every day. Many of the women take temporary work. The jobs tide them over until they make it to the big time. For most, there is no big time. If they get lucky, they work as extras, nonspeaking parts which place them among a sea of anonymous faces. Casting directors eyeball them and accept or reject them on a whim. When fame eludes them, the smart ones return home.

A few women refuse to throw in the towel, and sometimes their tenacity pays off with a career in TV or the movies. Others cling to their dreams and exist on the fringes of show business. Those women too often find themselves in potentially dangerous situations, socializing with questionable characters, doing things they would never dream of doing in their hometowns.

Jean Spangler

Cecil Martin Spangler and Florence Morris marry in Seattle, Washington, on February 21, 1918. By 1930, the couple live in Los Angeles with their four children: Richard, eleven; Betsy Ann, nine; Edward, eight; and Jean, six. Cecil works as a car salesman and Florence is a stay-at-home mom.

During the 1940s, the Spanglers rent a home northeast of downtown in Highland Park. The homes are a mix of Victorian mansions on the hillsides and cozy early-twentieth-century bungalows on the flatlands. The Arroyo Seco (Spanish for "dry stream") runs along Highland Park's eastern border. It travels from Red Box Canyon in the Angeles National Forest, passes through Pasadena near the Rose Bowl stadium, and continues through Highland Park, Hermon, Montecito Heights, and Cypress Park. It ends at the confluence with the Los Angeles River near Elysian Park.

Highland Park resembles a midwestern small town more than it does anyone's idea of a Los Angeles suburb. Mom-and-pop businesses line the main streets of York and Figueroa. The town has its own movie palace, the Highland Park movie theater, which opens in March 1925, and shows first-run movies.

Jean Gets Married

On June 28, 1942, Jean and Dexter Benner wed at the Hollywood-Beverly Christian Church. *The Highland Park News-Herald* reports the bride wore a gown of "white slipper satin with sweetheart neckline, and large puffed sleeves. From a crown of white satin flowed a fingertip veil, which was bound with satin. She carried a shower bouquet of gardenias and white roses."

Instead of capturing one of the happiest days of her life, the newspaper photo of Jean shows a woman second-guessing her decision to marry. Her expression is somber, not joyous. Like many wartime marriages, Jean's marriage to Dexter does not survive. Jean cheats on him while he serves in the South Pacific. Their divorce is acrimonious, and they fight bitterly over custody of their daughter, Christine.

Wartime tragedy touches most families, and Jean's is no exception. Her brother, Edward, is missing and presumed dead in a June 2, 1944, bombing raid over Osaka, Japan. Following her divorce from Dexter, Jean lives with her widowed sister-in-law, Sophie, while she pursues an acting career.

Jean's Show-Biz Career

Even a woman as attractive as Jean struggles to break into the movies. She works as a dancer at a popular Hollywood nightclub, the Florentine Gardens. Until police clear him, the club's co-owner, Mark Hansen, is one of the early suspects in the Black Dahlia murder.

In July 1949, Hansen makes headlines again—not as a suspected killer, but as a victim. A buxom blonde, twenty-five-year-old aspiring striptease queen, Lola Titus, has delusions of Hollywood grandeur and a pistol. She hands Hansen naked photos of herself and strips for him. When he fails to make her dreams come true, she enters the bathroom of his bungalow and shoots him, critically wounding him.

Jean's relationship with Hansen is strictly employee/employer. Florentine Gardens's patrons run the gamut from Hollywood stars to mobsters. Jean knows it is among the best places to be seen by people who can advance her career. She features prominently in advertising for the Florentine's shows as she continues to model, appearing in magazines across the county.

Typecast, the leggy dancer struts through eight film roles from 1948 through 1949—none of them with a name credit. She appears in everything from a Three Stooges short, *Mummy's Dummies*, to feature-length films. Jean is noticed, but none of the parts give her an opportunity to show off her acting chops.

The Lady Vanishes

At 5:30 p.m. on Friday, October 7, 1949, Jean tells Sophie she plans to meet Dexter to discuss increasing her child support. After meeting with her ex-husband, she is going to a movie set for work. She offers no details.

Night shoots are unusual for Jean, and the wink she gives Sophie on her way out the door speaks volumes. Jean is up to something. Jean phones at 7:30 p.m. to say goodnight to Christine and asks Sophie not to wait up.

Sophie awakens the next morning and realizes Jean is not home. She phones police to make a missing persons report. Police advise Sophie to stay calm, suggesting Jean has run off with a man and will probably return on her own.

Sophie persists. LAPD Wilshire Division homicide detectives M. E. Tullock and William Brennan put out an all-points bulletin for Jean, describing her as five-eight, one hundred forty pounds, and wearing dark-green slacks, a wool blouse, and a white sport jacket.

Police check the studios where Jean allegedly works. None of them has a project with her, and none of them scheduled a night shoot for October 7.

The police question Dexter, who insists he last saw his ex-wife several weeks ago. His new wife, Lynn, confirms that she and Dexter spent the night of the 7th at home together.

An unnamed informant phones in a tip. He recalls seeing Jean eating hot dogs with a clean-cut young man in front of a Vine Street market about 10:30 Friday night. He stops to say hello, and Jean introduces him to her companion. The informant apologizes because he cannot recall the man's name. The clue fizzles when the man realizes he saw Jean on Thursday, not Friday night.

A clerk at a store near Jean's home notices her on Friday and tells police she appeared to be waiting for someone.

A gas station attendant, Art Rodgers, waits on a man and a woman in a blue-gray convertible early Saturday morning. The man buys gas, saying it is for a trip to Fresno. The woman, dressed like Jean, appears uncomfortable and presses herself against the passenger-side door. As they drive away, the woman shouts, "Have the police follow this car!"

The convertible roars off, and Rodgers phones police. Patrol cars arrive too late to pick up the pair's trail.

A local radio personality, Al "the Sheik" Lazar, sees Jean at midnight on the 7th at the Cheese Box restaurant on Sunset Boulevard. She is sitting in a booth with two men. According to Lazar, she and the men argue. Despite the angry words and gestures, Jean leaves with them a little past midnight. The investigation reveals that Jean hits several more Sunset Strip night spots accompanied by a tall, handsome man whom none of her acquaintances recognize.

On October 9, two days after Jean's disappearance, thirty-five-year-old Henry Anger, a Griffith Park custodian, finds Jean's purse lying in the dirt near the Fern Dell entrance. It wasn't there when he made his rounds at 7:30 the night before. It is damaged, the double handles torn loose from the frame, but the contents, including her lucky silver dollar, are intact.

Anger finds identification in the bag. He calls the number and speaks with Sophie, then he phones police. They dispatch a radio car to Griffith Park. Examining the contents of the bag, police find an unfinished note addressed to "Kirk"—no surname. The note reads: "Can't wait any longer, going to see Dr. Scott. It will work best this way while mother is away."

Jean's mother, Florence, is visiting her son Richard in Lexington, Kentucky, when Jean goes missing. When Florence returns from her trip, reporters ambush her, shouting questions.

Florence sobs, "I can't imagine what has happened to Jeannie. I never heard of this Dr. Scott or Kirk. Something terrible must have happened to my little girl."

She later recalls that a Kirk picked Jean up twice and informs police. Each time Kirk stays in his car and waits for Jean to come out. Florence thinks his behavior is odd. A gentleman comes to the door. Does Kirk have something to hide?

The authorities search for Kirk, and they question every doctor in Los Angeles with the first or last name of Scott. None of them admit to having Jean as a patient.

Investigators uncover Jean's wartime affair during her marriage to Dexter. Her lover—a good-looking army lieutenant she calls "Scotty"— is jealous, with a nasty temper. He beats her and threatens to kill her if she leaves him. She ends the affair. Jean's lawyer tells police that, as far as he knows, Scotty left Los Angeles in 1945, and took his rage with him.

Young Man with a Horn

The unknown Kirk is a person of interest. The police discover that Jean has a small part in the Warner Brothers feature film *Young Man with a Horn*, starring Kirk Douglas. They think nothing of it until Douglas makes a preemptive call to deny knowing Jean. They wonder if the star has something to hide.

In a subsequent interview, Douglas admits he lied. He knows Jean, but she is a casual acquaintance—nothing more. Sure, he and Jean shared a few laughs on the set, but it is nothing out of the ordinary. He is friendly with all the actors and crew. When detectives ask where he was on October 7, he tells them he spent the weekend in Palm Springs with an entourage.

Kirk says, "I told Detective Chief Thad Brown that I didn't remember the girl or the name until a friend recalled it was she who worked as an extra in a scene with me in my picture *Young Man with a Horn*. Then I recalled she was a tall girl in a green dress. I talked and kidded with her a bit on the set, as I have done with many other people around on a day of shooting. But I never saw her before or after that and have never been out with her."

Police and reporters are skeptical of Kirk's explanation, which sounds rehearsed.

Just days before Jean vanishes, on the set of the movie *The Petty Girl*, actor Robert Cummings remembers seeing her. She is smiling and whistling.

"You sound happy."

She tells him about a new romance.

"Is it serious?"

She laughs. "Not exactly, but I'm having the time of my life."

Jean does not reveal the name of her new man.

Sinister Parallels

Newspapers opine on the "sinister parallels" between Elizabeth Short's 1947 murder and Jean's disappearance. On October 12, 1949, the *Long Beach Independent* sees similarities between the two young women. "Like the Black Dahlia, Jean was a frequenter of the gay Los Angeles and Hollywood night spots and was known as a laughter-loving beauty, always in the company of a date."

The *Los Angeles Daily News* reports that the police "were more than half convinced that if they do find the girl's body, it too may be mutilated—as was the body of Elizabeth Short, 'the Black Dahlia,' when it was found tossed into the weeds on a vacant lot in January 1947." The newspaper went further: "Like the Black Dahlia, the lost TV glamour girl was always willing, perhaps too willing, to make a sudden, impulsive date with a stranger, regardless of danger."

Implicit in the coverage is that Jean's behavior causes her disappearance because she is "too willing." The pejorative putdown of Jean's lifestyle is standard for the era.

A friend of Jean's tells police that Jean confided in her that she was three months pregnant and talked about having an illegal operation—a euphemism for an abortion. After talking to several people who frequent the same bars and nightclubs as Jean, police learn of a former medical student known as "Doc" who performs abortions for money. The police float the theory that Jean saw him to end her pregnancy and then suffered complications, which killed her. They cannot locate Doc or anyone willing to say they know him.

Mob Connections

Like many Hollywood performers, Jean has ties to local mobsters. At the Florentine Gardens, she rubs elbows with club regulars, such as underworld figure Mickey Cohen and his associates, like David "Little Davy" Ogul. Davy and Jean date. It is a mutually beneficial arrangement. Davy gets a beautiful woman on his arm, and Jean gains entrance into glamorous nightclubs she cannot afford on her own.

Davy oozes bad-boy charisma. He is under indictment and faces prison for conspiracy. Are Jean and Davy serious, or is he the guy with whom she is having the time of her life?

In September 1949, news of a sex extortion ring headed by Mickey Cohen makes front-page news. One complainant, thirty-nine-year-old Ben Kleckner, a Hollywood talent school operator, paid thousands of dollars to a twenty-six-year-old woman, Helen Keller, to buy her silence.

Caught up in the extortion ring is a onetime actor's agent, Paul Behrmann. Behrmann formerly represented actor Robert Mitchum. In August 1948, Mitchum is separated from his wife and partying in Laurel Canyon with actress Lila Leeds; her roommate, dancer Vicki Evans; and bartender-turned-real-estate-agent Robin Ford. On a tip, LAPD busts up the party and takes the quartet into custody for possession of marijuana.

Mitchum serves fifty days at a Los Angeles County honor farm. He poses for a staged photo in his jail blues, holding a mop. Rather than destroying his career, the drug bust enhances his outlaw image and his film career thrives until his death in 1997.

Jean and Ogul— Partners in Crime?

The extortion racket nets Cohen thousands of dollars. What if Davy and Jean run their own game on the QT? The couple spend their evenings together club-hopping. It is easy for Jean to cozy up to Hollywood producers, directors, and actors, maneuver them into a compromising situation, and then blackmail them.

At twenty-six, in a town where thirty is over the hill for a woman, Jean reaches a turning point. She has yet to receive a name credit for any of her film performances. For someone with ambition, being relegated to crowd scenes, dancer in a nightclub, and other underwhelming roles is career purgatory.

Davy is Jean's wise-guy equivalent—always the muscle, never the boss. Did he imagine a grander role for himself in the local underworld?

Jean's last two projects before her disappearance put her near Kirk Douglas and Robert Cummings. Kirk's reputation as a womanizer is common knowledge. There is no doubt he notices the shapely brunette bit-player. He admits to police that he spoke to her. Did Jean and Davy devise a honey trap for the actor?

"Jimmy the Weasel" Fratianno

On Labor Day weekend 1949, Frank Niccoli, one of Cohen's henchmen, phones his boss to say he received a dinner invitation from Jimmy Fratianno. Fratianno works for Cohen's nemesis, longtime Los Angeles crime boss Jack Dragna. After a few days, Cohen becomes worried about Niccoli and telephones Fratianno, who denies having seen him.

When Davy disappears in early October, Cohen says, "I'm afraid the guys ain't living. They was swallowed up."

In 1977, the Feds bust Fratianno, and he turns on his Mob pals. He confesses to several murders—including that of Frank Niccoli. He tells FBI investigators the gruesome details of the 1949 murder.

Niccoli arrives at Fratianno's apartment for dinner. A few minutes later, Joseph Dippolito, another Dragna stooge, arrives. Niccoli reaches over to shake Joe Dip's hand. Joe grabs him in a bear hug. Future Los Angeles Mob boss, Nick Licata, and brothers Carmen and Sam Bruno, all members of Dragna's gang, enter the room with a piece of rope. Fratianno wraps the rope around Niccoli's neck and holds on while Sam grabs the other end and pulls. Fratianno says, "Frankie, your time is up."

After choking Niccoli to death, the mobsters strip him, stuff the body in a mail sack, and throw it into the back of their car. They drive out to Dippolito's winery in Cucamonga, a favorite Mob boneyard, and dump the sack with the body, followed by a sack of lime, into a pre-dug hole.

Cohen was right about Niccoli, but what happened to Davy?

Fratianno confesses to five murders. He never mentions Davy. There is no reason for him to be coy about a sixth homicide. If Fratianno didn't kill Davy, who did?

Cohen Orders a Hit?

Earlier, I posited that Jean and Davy may have masterminded their own Hollywood extortion racket without Mickey Cohen's permission. If they struck out on their own and Cohen found out, he may have ordered a hit on them. Old-school mobsters hesitated to kill women, but that does not mean they never did.

Jean and Ogul Stayed Here

As in any high-profile disappearance, theories about Jean and Davy's whereabouts are legion. Without bodies or crime scenes, everything about their disappearances is speculation.

In 1950, a customs agent in El Paso, Texas, reports seeing Davy and a woman who strongly resembles Jean checking into a local hotel. A clerk at the hotel identifies Jean from a photo. A person matching Frank Niccoli's description accompanies the pair. The scenario holds together in 1949, but falls apart in 1977 with Jimmy Fratianno's confession.

Jean's story recalls the classic film noir *Out of the Past*, starring Robert Mitchum and Kirk Douglas. Mitchum crosses a vindictive mobster, Kirk Douglas, and he and a woman from his past end up dead.

Is that how it was for Jean and Davy? Did they cross Mickey Cohen and pay with their lives? Was Jean collateral damage in a hit on Davy, or was she taken by a monster, like the Black Dahlia slayer, as the newspapers speculated? Did the mysterious Kirk, the father of her unborn child, kill her?

Unlike *Out of the Past*, this story has no ending.

Austria's Most Wanted: Twenty-Seven Years and Counting

Iris Reinbacher

The spectacular case of Tibor Foco has captured the imagination of the Austrian public for decades. His conviction for murder after a highly publicized trial, and his meticulously planned escape from prison nine years later, have sparked debate about the Austrian justice system as a whole and, to this day, invite speculation as to what really happened all those years ago in 1986.

According to friends, Elfriede Hochgatter was a beautiful young woman, friendly and nice to everyone, but at the same time quite headstrong. She doted on her two younger brothers and regularly returned to her hometown, where she loved playing cards and board games with her family and devouring her mother's handmade sweets, a staple of Austrian food. In short, she was a normal, fun-loving, twenty-three-year-old woman. Yet Elfriede had a secret she carefully kept from her loved ones: she worked as a prostitute in the red-light district of Linz, Austria's third largest city. Sadly, they would find out about her secret life soon enough. Elfriede's murder shook the small town she came from just as much as it shook her family, and her father never recovered from the blow. But more than that, her violent death led to a spectacular trial, with allegations of a police setup and accusations of a miscarriage of justice.

And, as a side product, it created Austria's most famous fugitive, who is still on the run to this day.

A Violent Murder, an Obvious Suspect

In the early morning of March 14, 1986, a rail commuter on the way to Linz spotted a body from the train window and alerted the police. They arrived at the scene by the rail tracks around 6:45 a.m. and found the mutilated body of a young woman. She had been beaten so viciously, she had multiple bones in her arms and upper body broken before finally being killed with a revolver shot to the face. The fact that she was found naked from the waist down at once suggested a sex crime.

The police worked surprisingly swiftly. The dead woman's identity was soon determined, as was her profession as a prostitute. Elfriede Hochgatter's workplace, a bar called "Diskret," was less than two hundred meters from where her body had been discovered. Her blood was found on the street just outside the bar. Everything pointed to a crime in the red-light district, and the search for a suitable suspect started there. It didn't take long. The day after the murder, Tibor Foco was arrested.

Thirty-year-old Tibor Foco was the owner of the "Bunny" bar right next to the Diskret, which had similar offerings. He was not your ordinary pimp, however. He was born into a fairly well-to-do family in Linz (his father owned a photography studio) that had roots in Hungary. His first love was motorsports and fast cars—so much so that he wanted to become a professional motorcycle racer. And his dream came true. In the 1970s, Tibor became very successful in the European motorcycle championships. But even though he had a good career in sports and was well-liked, described by many as charming and intelligent, he opened a bar in Linz's red-light district.

Although prostitution is legal in Austria, it remains a shady business. Nevertheless, it is said that Tibor tried his best to run his establishment as much "above ground" as possible, with no bribes or other favors for the police and no involvement in petty crime or the sleazy internal politics of the red-light district. He was a newcomer trying to do things his own way. No wonder Tibor was eyed suspiciously by those in the district and stayed on the margins of the business. It's hard to understand why such a promising and successful young man would choose this particular lifestyle. Some suggest it may have been a calculated move purely for financial reasons, chiefly to support his motorsport career.

The police soon found out that, on the night of Elfriede Hochgatter's death, she and Tibor had a run-in that got out of hand. Apparently, he wanted to hire her services, either for a one-off personal *tête-à-tête*—something he was widely known for—or long-term for his business. Either way, she refused, and a verbal fight turned into a physical altercation. The police believed this was enough of a motive to make Tibor Foco a serious suspect, even though his wife gave him an alibi by saying he was home at the time when the murder was supposed to have taken place.

Along with Tibor, the police arrested Regina Ungar, his mistress. She also worked as a prostitute in his "Bunny" bar and was suspected of being his accomplice. All through March, she was questioned extensively by the police and gave varying accounts on what had happened that night. She finally stated that, not only had she been present at the murder, but Tibor had guided her hand and forced her to shoot Elfriede, threatening that otherwise she would end up dead as well. In early April, Regina Ungar once again changed her testimony. She now named Hans-Peter Löffler, a leather goods merchant from Linz, as another accomplice in the murder.

From Investigation to Verdict

After a lengthy police investigation that took almost a year, the trial finally started in February 1987. The facts seemed clear: even though Elfriede had been found naked from the waist down, a sex crime was ruled out very early. Blood and semen found on the body did not match Tibor Foco's, and there had been no gunshot residue on his hands when he was arrested. Although Tibor's wife, who had also been arrested and spent a few days in prison, retracted the alibi she had given him, and although Regina Ungar's final testimony had severely incriminated him, there was no hard physical evidence to connect him to the crime, or even the crime scene. And Tibor himself never confessed to the crime. On the contrary, throughout the months of investigation, the trial, and long afterward, he maintained his innocence.

But it didn't matter. It appeared that the trial was less concerned with finding the facts and the true murderer than it was with satisfying the media hype. Sex sells, and a local celebrity turned perverted sex murderer sold even more so. Tibor Foco's background, his unorthodox lifestyle, his views on women, and his sexual preferences in particular became an unexpected focal point both in court and in the media. Gruesome photos of the victim's body were shown in court, and an expert witness had gone so far as to taxidermically preserve Elfriede's facial skin and bring it with him to aid in his testimony. The jurors turned away in disgust, but the macabre spectacle was happily exploited by the media, including tabloids and serious newspapers alike. Even at the official visit to the crime scene, which had barely enough space to accommodate those involved, the press was present. Afterward, detailed photos and even video recordings circulated widely. In hindsight, all this seems deliberate, as if to distract from the nonexistent evidence—a conviction by public opinion rather than by irrefutable facts.

The trial took twenty days, in which the court heard seventy witnesses and five experts. The verdict was announced on March 31, 1987. Tibor Foco received a life sentence. His alleged accomplice Hans-Peter Löffler was sentenced to eighteen years in prison. Regina Ungar, who acted as the chief witness for the prosecution, was found not guilty since she had been forced to pull the trigger against her will, and thus acted under duress. After the trial, Tibor Foco was incarcerated in Stein near Linz, one of only three high-security prisons in Austria.

Case Closed– Not Everybody Happy

With Tibor Foco convicted of Elfriede Hochgatter's murder and safely locked away, interest in the case should have died down quickly. But it did not. Soon after the trial was over, doubts about Tibor's guilt were raised, and parts of the police investigation were questioned publicly. For example, while the semen that was found on Elfriede Hochgatter's body was ruled out as being Tibor Foco's, no effort was made to find the man to whom it actually belonged. Police simply declared it an inevitable part of a prostitute's occupation and left it at that.

It was also discovered that Elfriede had become unusually nervous and withdrawn in the weeks before her death. She had even taken out life insurance of more than 100,000 Austrian schillings (around €7,300), listing her younger brothers as beneficiaries. It is thought that she wanted to leave the business, yet was forced to stay. Why? And by whom? Again, the police did not investigate this further.

With Tibor Foco such a suitable and convenient suspect, it's not clear whether any attempt was made to look for other potential murderers. Elfriede's boyfriend at the time was questioned, and apparently his alibi for the night of the murder fell apart. However, there was no further investigation as to his possible involvement in his girlfriend's death. He later made off with Elfriede's life insurance money, leaving her brothers with nothing.

The behavior of Tibor's legal counsel also leaves plenty of room for questions. Apparently, he was advised by his lawyer to fully cooperate with the police investigation. Although Tibor always swore that he was innocent, there are photos from the crime scene visit where he and Regina Ungar together hold a revolver, pointing it at the head of a stand-in for Elfriede. The public was informed and, of course, shocked to see this. Obviously, the mid-1980s were different times, but what lawyer worth his salt would let his client incriminate himself like this, regardless of whether he believed him to be innocent?

After the trial had ended, jurors came forward and accused the judge of deliberately misleading them regarding the interrogation of Elfriede's boyfriend. Some had even visited Tibor in prison, and the prison director also believed him to be innocent. By now Tibor was divorced; his former wife later married one of the police officers involved the case. This did raise some eyebrows, but the newlywed couple denied having had an intimate relationship prior to the murder. Once again, there was no further inquiry.

In October 1989, one of the police officers who had investigated the case shot himself. Of course, a lot can happen in two and a half years, and the causes of suicides are generally hard to pinpoint. However, this particular suicide happened so soon after the filming of a documentary on the case had been finished that his colleagues believed there was a connection. But the internal affairs department did not, and the investigation into the suicide was closed rather quickly.

Interestingly, many of the accusations of police misconduct and various other issues surrounding the trial revolved around one police officer: Othmar Kreutzer. He was the one who repeatedly questioned Regina Ungar, who had implicated Tibor Foco only after days of interrogation and changed her testimony seven times in total. In court,

Kreutzer testified that he had never been alone with her even though official records of the interrogations showed otherwise. He was caught lying again regarding letters Ungar had sent to a friend, which were confiscated by the police. Records of the search conducted at her friend's house do not mention any letters. When Kreutzer was asked about them during the trial, he testified that the police had seized many letters, but he couldn't recall how many had been written by Ungar, if indeed, any were at all.

However, the biggest bomb did not explode until 1993, six years after Foco and Löffler were convicted. Chief witness Regina Ungar, who had formerly claimed that Tibor had forced her to kill Elfriede, withdrew her testimony. From the safety of her new residence in the United States, she now asserted that police officer Kreutzer had beaten and tortured her during the initial questioning. She even said that he dictated her final "confession," then forced her to sign it, and that he was always close by at the crime scene visit, making sure she made no wrong moves.

One would assume such a revelation would lead to an instant retrial, but justice is notoriously slow in Austria and elsewhere. It took three more years until, in 1996, Tibor's alleged accomplice, Hans-Peter Löffler, who stated that he never even knew why he was tried in the first place, was acquitted. Several more years of lawsuits against the Austrian state went by before he eventually received compensation of 4.4 million Austrian schillings (roughly €320,000) for the ten years he'd spent in prison as an innocent man.

On the other hand, Tibor Foco, who continued to maintain his innocence, had all his petitions for a retrial denied and remained imprisoned in Stein. As the only Austrian prisoner serving a life sentence given permission to study at university, he studied law at the Johannes Kepler University in Linz. At first, he conducted his studies via distance learning and was only allowed to go to university for his exams. Because of his effort and high grades, and because of interventions by professors who took a liking to their student, he was later allowed to attend selected lectures in person, always accompanied by police officers. This unprecedented decision would be his lucky break.

Minutiae of an Escape

On April 27, 1995, Tibor Foco attended a lecture at Kepler University. He arrived with two policemen around 8:25 a.m., which left plenty of time to have a coffee and take a seat in the lecture hall before the lecture began. Tibor and one of his guards—the other waited in a car outside—went to the lecture hall on the third floor of the law building, where Tibor left his bag. He and his guard then went to the main building, Tibor ostensibly wanting to use the toilet there. On arriving, he claimed that he needed to "check something" in lecture hall number one. Tibor went through one door, turned a corner, quickly left through another door, and promptly disappeared in the early-morning bustle of the university.

The police officer who accompanied Tibor was dumbfounded. After years of his prisoner's exemplary conduct, the officer had not expected him to run. When he couldn't find him, he informed his colleague, and soon a large-scale search was underway. But, by the time reinforcements arrived and police helicopters circled above the university and the neighborhood, Tibor Foco was long gone.

As the police would ascertain later, Tibor's escape had been planned for years, with the prisoner himself the mastermind. He had recruited family members, old friends from his motorsport years, and even female acquaintances he had made while in prison, to help. From as early as 1993, mobile phones had been smuggled into his cell; from then on, he could freely and secretly communicate with the outside world. Friends scouted out the university buildings and surroundings, took photos of quiet crossroads that went through fields, and planned the fastest routes leading away from the city. All necessary equipment was prepared and hidden in prearranged places. On that April morning, everything was ready to go.

After Tibor Foco had shaken off his guard in the main building, he ran back to the law building, where a key to a nearby rental garage had been placed in a toilet stall. He made his way to the garage, where the necessities for his flight were hidden: an unregistered mobile phone, a fake passport, 500,000 Austrian schillings in cash (€35,000), plus a few days' worth of provisions, clothing, and, most importantly, a motorcycle with a full tank of fuel and a fake number plate. Tibor put on the leather gear and helmet and drove off. In less than ten minutes, he had gone from model prisoner to fugitive on the run.

Despite the large-scale search that had begun immediately after his disappearance, the trail went cold. The police were able to reconstruct the first part of the escape, but Tibor's tracks were soon lost in the busy city. It is thought that he first made his way to the Czech Republic, the border being less than an hour from Linz. From there he may have traveled on to Hungary, where he had family. Nothing is certain. Rumors have placed Tibor in numerous countries all over the world, from Eastern Europe to South America and Southeast Asia. According to the latest gossip, he works as a truck driver and is the father of two children. But what really happened to him after he rode his motorcycle into rush-hour traffic that April morning, no one knows for sure.

No Turning Back

Tibor Foco's spectacular escape caused an enormous uproar in Austria. He was immediately placed on the "Austria's Most Wanted" list, and the media spotlight was on him once more. The murder case was rehashed in detail, and now included all the new allegations against the police and the justice system that had surfaced in the eight years since the trial. In 1997, one year after the acquittal of Hans-Peter Löffler, Tibor's sentence was repealed and a retrial mandated. According to Austrian law, it is illegal to try a person in their absence. Therefore, from spring 1997 to October 1, 1997, the international arrest warrant was retracted and Tibor Foco was offered safe conduct upon his return to Austria. However, he did not take up the offer, and he remained missing.

It was around this time that the case became political. Between 1997 and 2005, dozens of parliamentary interpellations to the Minister of Justice and the Minister of the Interior were placed by members of various political parties. These concerned issues such as alleged police misconduct, police torture, and the mishandling of evidence, and they sought to find evidence for possible deeper-lying problems in the Austrian judicial and police system. However, the answers given by the respective and ever-changing ministers were brief at best and evasive at worst. They frequently cited the once-again open trial and other legal procedures that couldn't be interfered with or even publicly discussed.

Over time, more and more inconsistencies in the case came to light. Crucial evidence had disappeared, a fact the prosecution ascribed to several relocations of the evidence room over the years. The questioning of Elfriede's boyfriend during the trial, which was conducted outside of court with only the judge present, was found to have been illegal. Although years earlier the jurors had complained about the judge misleading them about this questioning, the judge never faced legal consequences or disciplinary action.

And neither did Officer Kreutzer, who, on top of all his previous lies in the Tibor Foco trial, allegedly blackmailed a witness to perjure himself in the Hans-Peter Löffler trial. Kreutzer's extensive personal connections to the underworld in Linz had now become public knowledge and were heavily scrutinized. For instance, he was close friends with the owner of a bar in the red-light district—so close, in fact, he served as best man at the bar owner's wedding. If Tibor had indeed made enemies in the demimonde because of his new business style, as it was alleged, it isn't unthinkable that Kreutzer was asked for a favor or two by his friends.

Yet none of these allegations against Kreutzer was ever substantiated, and even his outright lies during the first trial didn't lead to any disciplinary action. While the investigators did find discrepancies in several records involving Kreutzer, they ascribed them to unwitting departures from compulsory procedures, which often happens in daily practice. Although Tibor's parents attempted to sue Kreutzer over Regina Ungar's lost letters—which they believed would prove their son's innocence—the case was dismissed early on and never went to trial.

In 2000, Tibor Foco was once again officially charged with the murder of Elfriede Hochgatter. The prosecution cited new evidence for their decision: the pink nail polish on Elfriede's exhumed body matched minute particles found under the fingernails of both Tibor and Regina. Also, dog hairs found on Elfriede's coat were a match to the dogs Tibor owned at the time of the crime. Of course, it's also possible these particles were transferred during the fight Tibor and Elfriede had on the night of her murder. As such, this doesn't seem to warrant renewed charges, particularly since Regina Ungar's withdrawn testimony didn't lead to an instant retrial. In any case, without Tibor Foco present in court, the trial could not proceed, and it has been on hold ever since.

Five years later, Tibor's parents intervened with the Minister of Justice, asking for the charges to be dropped completely. However, in a high-profile case like this, it was inadvisable from a political point of view. Instead, the minister at the time made another offer of safe conduct, which again Tibor did not take up.

The Impact of a Murder

Elfriede Hochgatter's murder and Tibor Foco's escape remain one of the most notorious crimes in Austria's recent history. Virtually every Austrian knows the name Tibor Foco, which may be due to the continued media attention he receives, especially around anniversaries of his escape. The case also keeps inspiring creative artists.

In 2020, a play named *Casting Tibor Foco* was planned to be staged, but had to be postponed due to the COVID-19 pandemic. That same year, a female accomplice to the escape, who called herself "Trudy Truth," published a tell-all book on how she became romantically involved with Tibor and how they, together with others, planned his escape.

In 2007, the TV film *Die Geschworene* (*The Juror*) was made with Austrian film star Christiane Hörbiger in the title role of a juror who has doubts after convicting a man who is sentenced to life in prison. While all the names and some details were changed, the film leaned heavily on the facts of the Foco case and has done much to influence public opinion. Today, most Austrians—including Elfriede's mother—believe Tibor Foco to be an innocent victim of a police setup.

Despite continued interest in the case, there is no well-researched book about it. Not even Austria's best-known investigative journalists have touched the topic. Is it still too hot after all these years? Is there someone in the background preferring that it be left alone? The more time passes, the more difficult it will be to separate fact from fiction. The official files are not accessible to the general public, understandably so since the case has been reopened; plus many of the people involved are now retired or have died, like Tibor's parents.

Tibor Foco still features on Interpol's most-wanted list. Remaining on the run since 1995, he has become Austria's longest-missing fugitive. The police are still actively searching for him and regularly publish new, digitally aged photographs of Tibor, who turned sixty-six in 2022. Yet it's very unlikely he will ever be found. Even during his time in prison, he stood out as a man who kept a strict daily schedule and was extremely disciplined, both mentally and physically. These are very useful traits for someone who wants to go into hiding and stay hidden for good.

What really happened that night in March 1986? Did Tibor Foco kill Elfriede Hochgatter in a fit of rage? Or was she murdered because of some internal feud in the red-light district, and Tibor had to take the fall for it? Who knows? Regina Ungar probably knows, but she made it clear that she will only reveal the truth on her deathbed. Tibor Foco knows for sure, but he doesn't want to be found—if he is even still alive. And anyone else who knows the truth is unlikely to come forward after all these years. By now, the truth has taken a back seat for good. So the spotlight remains on Tibor Foco, leaving the real victim, Elfriede Hochgatter, disregarded and forgotten in the shadows.

The Curious Case of the Dogs in the Nighttime: France's "Valley of Hell" Mystery

Dean Jobb

The body of a woman, clad in nightclothes, was found floating in a water tank behind her villa in western Provence. There was a bullet hole in her forehead and a revolver—*her* revolver—was fished from the bottom of the cistern; it had fired a single round. Olive Branson, a wealthy English artist in her mid-forties, could have been the victim of a botched robbery. A spurned lover or a vindictive neighbor might have shot her, then tried to hide her body. Yet the first police officer on the scene, Captain Fabre from the nearby town of St. Rémy, compared notes with a doctor who examined the body and reached a startling conclusion. On the night of April 26, 1929, Branson had dressed for bed, stepped outside, climbed into the cistern, stood up to her neck in cold water, and shot herself.

In England, relatives and friends were incredulous. Her prominent and well-connected family (a cousin, Sir George Arthur Harwin Branson—the grandfather of billionaire Sir Richard Branson—was a High Court judge) demanded that the case be reopened. Olive wintered in Provence but had been in London barely a week before she died for a brief visit and a dental appointment. "She appeared to be in general good health and spirits," Lady Branson, the judge's wife, assured a *Manchester Guardian* reporter who turned up at their estate in Surrey. "I think that the idea of suicide can be 'washed out' altogether. There was nothing at all suicidal about her."

The police force in Marseilles, the largest city in the region, dispatched one of its top detectives to take a second look. Chief Inspector Alexandre Guibbal was convinced there was a simpler, more logical explanation for the death. He arrived with a forensics team a week after the body was found, and soon found traces of blood inside the villa. A trail of bloodstains led outside to the cistern. Guibbal examined Branson's stockings and could see no tears to the fabric, suggesting she had not walked across the graveled courtyard—she had been carried out of the house.

This was no suicide. Branson had been murdered.

The isolated villa was three-quarters of a mile from the Rhône Valley village of Les Baux-de-Provence. Branson's servants, who lived on the grounds, and her neighbors reported hearing a gunshot about 8:45 that evening. Strangely, no one seemed to have been alarmed and no one investigated. More intriguing, for Guibbal, was what had not been heard. Branson's four dogs had been locked in a pen about thirty feet from the cistern, but none of them had barked during the night.

In Arthur Conan Doyle's Sherlock Holmes story "The Adventure of Silver Blaze," his super-sleuth deduced why a guard dog did not bark on the night a racehorse was stolen. The "curious incident of the dog in the night-time," as Holmes famously described it, was proof that the thief was someone familiar, and not a stranger.

Guibbal, like the great detective of fiction, understood the significance of the silent dogs. The animals must have known and recognized her killer. It could be the clue he needed to crack the case.

———

Alfred Munnings thought she "could draw like a wizard." A painter and war artist acclaimed for his depictions of rural scenes, magnificent horses, and life behind the front lines during the First World War, Munnings met Olive Branson at a summer school for artists and remembered her as "the kindest and sweetest person." Each fall, she wandered the Hampshire countryside with caravans of Romani people, recording their lives in ink as they moved from camp to camp to harvest hops. She invited Munnings to join her, and he produced idyllic portraits of their encampments—children at play, men at work with their horses, wagons and tents creating temporary villages beside the hedgerows. Branson camped in comfort and style, in a covered wagon decorated with elaborate carvings and gilding, and hired a groom to tend to her horses. But she was a "true Bohemian," in the words of a Munnings biographer, who befriended her fellow travelers and fit in.

Edith May Olive Branson was born in 1885 and grew up in India, where her father practiced law. Her parents died when she was young, and she moved to London with an inheritance that freed her to pursue her passion for art. "Although she was not wealthy," noted her cousin's wife, Lady Branson, "she was comfortably off." Besides her portrayals of Romani life, Branson drew female nudes and produced lifelike studies of greyhounds. In 1913, the renowned British chemist Sir Thomas Edward Thorpe commissioned her to illustrate a memoir of his yachting excursions on the Seine; critics judged her drawings to be one of the highlights of the book. Her "delicate and suggestive illustrations," in the opinion of *The Contemporary Review*, enhanced "the value of the book in every way." Branson's appearance was as attractive and elegant as her drawings. She wore her hair in a fashionable bob, parted on the right side. When she posed for a studio photograph that would one day appear in newspapers around the world, she wrapped herself in an elegant fur shawl, clutched a thin walking stick, and offered the camera the slightest of smiles.

Twenty-nine when war broke out in 1914, she joined the Women's Army Auxiliary Corps and did volunteer work for the YMCA and the Red Cross. She became engaged to a French officer, but he was killed in action before they could marry. In July 1918, she married Major Arthur Ernest Wilson, a British Army officer she was said to have met in the midst of a German air raid on their base. The couple honeymooned in Cornwall but separated after only a fortnight together. The marriage was not formally dissolved, however, until 1927. Wilson's friends, according to one press account, attributed the split to Branson's "eccentricities and strange mode of life." An independent woman who embraced a bohemian lifestyle and was building a career as an artist, it appears, was not a good match for a military man.

After the war, Branson spent part of each year in the South of France. She gravitated to the countryside near Arles, the historic city on the western edge of Provence where Van Gogh had lived and painted for a year in the 1880s. She bought Ciscaille, a modest villa near Les Baux. Built on a limestone outcrop overlooking the Rhône Valley, Les Baux had once been a town of four thousand, but over the centuries its chateau and most of its buildings had been abandoned. An aluminum-bearing ore discovered nearby in the early 1800s was christened bauxite in the village's honor, but the mineral deposit did not attract people or prosperity to the region. By the late 1920s, the *Baedeker's Guide* to Provence billed Les Baux as "a ruined and almost deserted town" with a population of about eighty. Each year, thousands of visitors arrived by automobile or train from Arles to stroll its almost-deserted streets and survey its crumbling ruins. After a local writer compared the hot, arid climate and weathered rock formations to something out of Dante's *Inferno*, the area became known as *Le Val de l'Enfer*—the Valley of Hell.

Branson was as comfortable in Les Baux as she had been when she camped with the Roma of Hampshire. She could speak French and wore the same broad-brimmed hats and flowing, pleated skirts as the local women. She converted a room of the villa into a studio and was often spotted hiking with her dogs in the rugged hills. She hired a local couple, the Girards, to help run the place—Joseph Girard as gardener, his wife as cook. She surprised her neighbors with presents and gift-wrapped toys for their children at Christmas. She even invested in the community's only industry, tourism, and bought a fourteen-bed hotel in the village, the Monte Carlo. It was a modest, one-story building that boasted a bar, café, and bistro tables set up in its tree-shaded courtyard. But her generosity may not have been enough to ingratiate her with residents who considered even Parisians to be *étrangers*—foreigners. "Les Baux is not France," observed one of the journalists parachuted in to cover Branson's death. "It is the Provence of the mountain villages, where often enough the mentality is still that of the Middle Ages." The real estate purchases may have earned her resentment, even enemies. "The love of the soil in the South is as hot and as fiery as the red earth of Provence," the journalist noted, "and 'foreigners' who buy even a scrap of that stony and sunbaked rock are not always looked upon with an indulgent eye."

One local man regarded Branson with far more than an indulgent eye. François Pinet was a twenty-seven-year-old whose father had owned and operated the Hôtel de Monte Carlo before Branson purchased it. He had a thin face and his dark, curly hair was receding, exposing a high forehead that made him look slightly older. While one press report described him as "very good-looking," other observers remarked on his blank expression, pale complexion, and a monotone speaking style that, like his face, betrayed no emotion. He was "a young man of honorable family and tolerably good character," *The Guardian* told its readers, "whose principal fault was his laziness." The three years of compulsory military service he completed after turning twenty exposed him to life outside Les Baux. He returned home to help his father run the hotel but appears to have taken little interest in the business. He headed for Marseilles "on pleasure bent" whenever he could, *The Guardian* noted, "and all of his capacities seem to have been devoted to obtaining the greatest amount of pleasure out of life with the least possible trouble."

In retrospect, it seems inevitable that Branson and Pinet would become lovers, despite the eighteen-year difference in their ages. She was alone in a remote area of a foreign country where he was one of the few bachelors to be found. After her fiancé's death and a brief, failed marriage, she appeared to have finally found the happiness that had eluded her. "He is delightfully simple and direct," she confided to her London friends. "He is young and he loves me. He is full of primitive passion but gentle as a lamb and absolutely in my control."

Pinet, for his part, wanted more out of life than the stifling, insular world of his home village, and Branson had the money to offer it; by 1929, her net worth was £29,000, the equivalent of almost USD $2.5 million today. He may have been in love with her, though had he known what she was saying about him, he may well have resented being described as docile and under her thumb. While it's not clear when the affair began, by the end of 1928 Branson had bought the hotel from Pinet's father and installed her lover as manager. If anything happened to her, Branson assured him, the hotel would be his and he would not lose his livelihood. In a letter written in French, dated December 2, 1928, and addressed to "My Dear Francois," she told him she would designate him the sole beneficiary in her will. "I shall bequeath you the Hôtel de Monte Carlo and also the estate," she promised. But it would be a long time, she added, before she was gone and Pinet could claim his inheritance. "By then," she joked, "I shall be a dear old thing of ninety."

————————

Chief Inspector Guibbal was considered "one of the cleverest detectives" in France. His work for the British intelligence service during the war won him accolades and a medal. With a homburg pushed back from his forehead and an oversized notebook stuffed into the pocket of his coat, he resembled a French version of Columbo. And like the disheveled television detective, he was relentless and refused to accept at face value what he saw and what he was told. One journalist described him as "a typical French detective of the new school," which seemed to mean that he preferred to carefully gather and assess evidence, not jump to conclusions.

Guibbal and his team scoured the villa in search of clues. A police photographer snapped images of the cistern, the doors and windows along the rear wall of the building, and the adjacent courtyard. Dr. Georges Béroud, a chemist and ballistics expert who accompanied them, was in charge of the Marseilles police laboratory and would later publish a textbook on forensic techniques. The Marseilles lab was considered one of the best in the country and was equipped with X-ray machines, spectrometers, and other cutting-edge devices that could tease clues out of samples collected at crime scenes. Béroud and his analysts had been instrumental in solving a recent double murder—their tests, which revealed that two firearms had been used, helped convict a second suspect who had denied his involvement in the killings.

Fortunately, the villa's entrances had been sealed, even though the local police had concluded it was not a crime scene. Guibbal, by one account, produced a powerful magnifying glass and got down on his hands and knees to scan the floor. He located a cluster of brown spots in Branson's bedroom, then followed a trail of tiny stains leading outside to the cistern. Béroud's tests would soon confirm it was human blood. The doctor felt it necessary to state the obvious to the growing number of reporters descending on Les Baux to cover the mysterious death. "It would be impossible," he assured them, "for a woman to have shot herself through the brain and then to have walked to the tank." To further discredit the suicide theory, the forensics team photographed the soles of Branson's stockings, then enlarged the photos to confirm the fabric was not torn or damaged. Guibbal had been right—she had not walked across the courtyard to the cistern.

An autopsy offered insights into how she was murdered. She had been shot execution-style, between the eyes and at point-blank range. The bullet's downward trajectory suggested the killer was taller or standing above her. There were no scrapes or bruises, tears to her clothing, or other evidence of a struggle, so it must have happened quickly, before she had time to react or to defend herself. A sponge found in the villa suggested the killer had cleaned up most of the blood, leaving only the telltale traces. The investigators examined the cistern, which sat atop a low wall and was difficult to reach. Someone with considerable strength had opened the heavy lid and pulled back a thick wire mesh to gain access. Since Guibbal doubted one person could have lifted the body inside without scraping the skin or tearing the nightdress, they could be looking for a murderer and an accomplice.

The Marseilles team spent three days gathering evidence and questioning witnesses. The "Valley of Hell" mystery became an international sensation, France's contribution to the crime-filled Roaring Twenties—a decade the French called *les Années folles* (the crazy years). Guibbal's investigation unfolded in the pages of newspapers as far away as Australia. In the United States, the *Brooklyn Daily Eagle* and other papers were astounded by the chief inspector's willingness to allow journalists to observe and monitor his work. News photographers snapped away as witnesses were interviewed. In a photo that was clearly staged for the press, Guibbal sat on the edge of the cistern and held a revolver awkwardly to his forehead as he conferred with Béroud. The Associated Press wire service distributed a report praising the lead investigator for taking "the French public into his confidence…. Instead of rumors and theories the public was always in possession of facts."

Branson's gardener, Joseph Girard, had found her body the day after she was shot. He recreated the discovery for Guibbal and, at some point, the detective realized that Girard's wife—Branson's cook—was the sister of François Pinet. Les Baux was indeed a small world, and village gossips no doubt confirmed that Pinet and Branson had been an item. Guibbal took Pinet and his brother-in-law into custody and subjected them to a grueling, seventeen-hour interrogation in Marseilles. Guibbal ruled out Girard as either a suspect or accomplice and focused his attention on Pinet. Bank records showed he was mired in debt and had received large sums from Branson. The money had been used to operate the hotel, he insisted. He denied they had been lovers, but Guibbal knew he was lying; employees of Marseilles hotels, shown photographs of the couple, had recognized them as guests who had checked in using assumed names. Confronted with this evidence, Pinet claimed he was guilty only of chivalry and trying to protect Branson's reputation. "He had lied like a gentleman," noted one news report, "because he had given his word never to reveal the romance."

Pinet also neglected to mention that he was about to become the new owner of the hotel. Branson's letter, promising to name him as her beneficiary, was found tucked into a compartment of his wallet. A search of his room at the hotel turned up a will in Branson's handwriting; drafted the previous December, it directed that he would inherit the property when she died.

Pinet refused to discuss the damning evidence, let alone confess. At one point during the interrogation, an exasperated Guibbal asked him to pretend, for a moment, that their roles were reversed. Pinet, now the detective, had discovered that his suspect, Guibbal, had lied about his relationship with the murder victim and concealed the fact he was named in the victim's will.

"After all that, what would you do in my place?" Guibbal asked.

"I should arrest you," Pinet acknowledged.

Did Guibbal, the real detective in the room, have enough evidence to make an arrest? He believed he had the right man, but he wanted to be certain. He bundled Pinet into a car and drove him to the villa to see if a return to the crime scene would loosen his tongue.

Branson's dogs were still in their kennel. When Guibbal got out of the car, they barked and snarled at the policeman, just as they would have if a stranger had entered the grounds on the night of the shooting. The moment they heard Pinet's voice, the animals fell silent.

"I do not know what you have against me," Pinet declared as a half-dozen journalists watched Guibbal place him under arrest. It was a good question. The dogs could not be called as witnesses. While the Marseilles police had plenty of evidence of murder, none of it directly connected Pinet to the crime. A thin veneer of circumstantial evidence, speculation, and rumor could not mask the holes in the prosecution's case.

Janet Flanner, *The New Yorker*'s Paris-based correspondent during the Jazz Age, once remarked on how odd France's criminal court procedures appeared to outsiders. "To Americans, it seems that French trials consist of two trials, with something being decided at the second one." That, in a nutshell, was how it worked. The first step was an investigative hearing to establish the evidence that would be presented during stage two, the trial before the jury that would ultimately decide whether a defendant was guilty. The court official who presided over the initial hearing was not an impartial judge; the *juge d'instruction* directed the police investigation, and subjected suspects and witnesses alike to blunt questioning in the pursuit of the truth.

Pinet's *juge d'instruction* was Monsieur Rochu, who relished his role as a devil's advocate. Rochu grilled him about the affair, the will, and the money he had received from Branson. Pinet acknowledged he was likely the last person, other than her killer, to see her alive. He had driven to the villa the evening she died to deliver milk and gasoline but said he had left about eight o'clock—at least forty-five minutes before the gunshot was heard. He claimed he was at the villa for no more than five minutes, but Rochu scoffed at the notion that Pinet had behaved like a delivery driver and had spent so little time with his lover.

At one point, Pinet mentioned "Miss Branson's enemies."

"Name them," Rochu demanded. "Whom do you suspect?" Pinet said nothing.

When the hearing wrapped up in August 1929, Rochu offered his version of what had happened the night Branson died. Pinet had driven to the villa to demand money. There were rumors Pinet was seeing another woman, and Branson had feared "he was going to give her up." They had argued. Pinet, "tired of the liaison" with an older woman, had lost his temper. "He seized Miss Branson's revolver…shot her dead, and threw her body in the well."

He asked Pinet if he had anything to say in response.

"I am innocent," he replied. "It was suicide."

––––––––––

By the time Pinet stood trial in January 1930, the woman found floating in a water tank had been tried and convicted in the press for her unconventional, independent lifestyle. The man accused of Branson's murder may have been reluctant to sully her reputation, but plenty of journalists were eager to do the job for him. The sexism and double standards of the time were on full display in widely distributed newspaper features that portrayed her as a seductress who had led an impressionable young Frenchman astray. "No girl was ever easier for a man to meet," noted a full-page account of the case published in the *San Francisco Examiner* and other papers only weeks after her death. "At parties she made it her business to become acquainted with every stranger, regardless of age, social rank, or of attractiveness." Another account made snide references to her apparent penchant for roaming London's streets at night to strike up an "acquaintanceship" with "the most casual passerby." Her long-ago forays into the countryside to sketch the Roma in their camps were presented as further evidence of her immorality and depravity. "The young woman…sometimes lived a week or more with the roaming bands," noted one writer who seemed to shudder at the thought. But being choosy, not promiscuous, seems to have been her real crime. Branson was "one of those ladies," in *The Philadelphia Inquirer*'s opinion, "whose restless spirits are goaded into seeking 'ideal love' in concrete masculine guise." She had "moved in social circles where she met men of culture and wealth," the writer of the *San Francisco Examiner* feature pointed out, "but spurned them all." She could have lived out her days as the respectable wife of a London banker or an English country squire; instead, she had stooped to a clandestine relationship with a poor man—a foreigner no less—who had likely taken her life. It was a concerted press campaign of victim-blaming; Branson's reckless behavior had culminated in her death.

The trial was staged in a three-centuries-old courthouse in Aix-en-Provence, with at least forty journalists on hand to flash the news via telephone and telegraph to Paris and, from there, to newspapers across the globe. Lawyers claimed the few remaining seats in the tiny courtroom as a frustrated crowd of would-be spectators—including a contingent that had journeyed from Les Baux—gathered outside. A squad of soldiers, with bayonets fixed to their rifles, surrounded the building to deter gate-crashers.

Pinet, wearing a blue suit and a polka-dot tie, was flanked by uniformed guards in the prisoner's dock. In another departure from British and American legal practice, the trial opened with *l'interrogatoire*—the judge's interrogation of the defendant. Pinet was combative and took exception to the judge's assertion that, short of money and deeply in debt, he had decided to improve his financial situation "by getting rid of Miss Branson."

"It's untrue, she killed herself," he insisted, doubling down on the dubious theory of suicide. "It would be far easier for Miss Branson to enter the cistern alive and then kill herself than it would be for anyone to place a dead body inside."

Dr. Béroud, however, testified that the discovery of bloodstains inside the villa made murder "a certainty." Dr. Cot, the first physician to examine the body, refused to budge from his verdict of suicide. He was handed Branson's revolver and, pressing the weapon to his forehead, demonstrated for the jury that it was possible to pull the trigger with his thumb. Captain Fabre, the police officer who was first on the scene, admitted his finding of suicide rested largely in the "calm and natural" expression on Branson's face and the fact her eyes were closed. One of the Marseilles police officers involved in the investigation offered a dubious explanation of why Pinet became a suspect—it was his assertion that he had dropped off supplies on the night of the murder and left within minutes. "No Frenchman would leave his mistress without taking a fond farewell, which would take time," Inspector Laforgue said, no doubt as some spectators nodded in agreement. "So we knew he was lying." Another doctor, shifting the focus to the victim's mental state, testified he had been treating Branson for "a nervous condition" since 1928.

The prosecutor, in his closing address, condemned Pinet as "an idler and a spendthrift." He offered the jury his theory of what had happened that night, which echoed the scenario set out by the examining magistrate. The relationship had soured, and Branson was planning to sell the hotel, throwing him out of work. Pinet went to the villa to ask for money; when she refused the request, he seized her revolver, shot her, and dumped her body and the firearm into the cistern.

At one point, with theatrical flourish, the prosecutor reminded the defendant that he faced the guillotine if convicted. "Pinet!" he shouted. "You still have a chance to confess now. I won't ask for the death sentence, but only for imprisonment." He pointed to the courtroom clock. "You have yet time!"

Pinet's lawyer responded with a stage-worthy performance of his own, stretching the evidence—as well as logic—to a breaking point. His client, "a young man of high moral standards," had found himself "enmeshed in the net of a siren." Branson was unstable, a "highly strung and temperamental woman," and he had become "a slave to her passion." She was convinced Pinet was about to abandon her "for a younger and prettier rival," and could not bear to live without him. A letter from the Royal Academy of Arts in London had arrived the day of her death, rejecting one of her paintings for an upcoming exhibition. Heartbroken over Pinet and devastated by the professional rebuke, she had taken her own life—and in a manner designed to make her lover look like her killer. "That, gentlemen," he told the all-male jury, "is the psychology of love."

The judge, in his summation, urged the jury to reject the suicide theory. Four medical experts had testified, and all but one had concluded Branson was murdered. The jurors either ignored their findings or did not believe there was enough evidence to implicate Pinet. Their verdict: not guilty. Pinet's supporters, relieved that one of their own had not been branded a murderer, burst into cheers, applause, and shouts of "*Vive Pinet!*" The defendant, who had been stoic throughout the trial—"as if wearing an iron mask," as one observer put it—burst into tears.

"She killed herself," he told journalists as he was set free after nine months in custody. "What else can I say?"

———————

"*Ni Crime, Ni Suicide,*" a headline in the French crime magazine *Détective* declared after the acquittal. But if Branson's death was neither a crime nor a suicide, what was it? The headline was misleading—a jury may have exonerated Pinet, but someone had committed a crime. The bloodstains found inside the villa proved she had been shot in her home, and the killer had carried her body outside and dumped it in the cistern. There was no evidence of a break-in, and nothing appeared to have been taken from the villa, making it unlikely she had been overpowered and shot by a burglar.

Guibbal had been correct to zero in on Pinet as the prime suspect. There was no evidence to suggest Branson had been the victim of a random attack. "In France," as veteran Paris correspondent Janet Flanner once told *Time* magazine, "nobody ever kills anyone he doesn't know." Pinet lied about his affair with Branson. He neglected to mention the will that left the hotel to him. He was no doubt lying when he claimed that the money he received from Branson was used to operate the hotel, not to line his pockets. His claim to have left the villa before the shooting was uncorroborated. His stubborn insistence that Branson had committed suicide, despite the overwhelming evidence of murder, seemed to scream of a desperate bid to escape punishment. And Branson's dogs knew and obeyed Pinet, explaining their silence on the night of the murder. The case against him, however, was circumstantial—no eyewitnesses, no forensic evidence linking him to the body or to the crime scene, no confession, despite Guibbal's long and vigorous interrogation. A sympathetic Provençal jury may have closed ranks to acquit one of their own, but the lack of evidence justified their verdict of not guilty.

Was there another explanation? Was Branson's death, *The Philadelphia Inquirer* wondered in the wake of the trial, "the most fiendishly ingenious 'spite suicide' of the twentieth century?" Did she kill herself, as the defense had claimed, to punish Pinet or as part of a plan to frame him for her murder? American psychologist Dr. William Marston, touted as an expert in criminal behavior, promoted this theory in a 1931 newspaper feature that promised to "debunk the 'scientific detective' methods" and expose "the human motives behind famous crimes." Branson, distraught over the end of the affair with Pinet, had "snuffed out her own life" as an act of revenge. "Any woman, young or old," Marston was convinced, "is quite capable, psychologically, of killing herself to injure the man who scorns her." The bizarre explanation was not the final word on Branson's death. In the mid-1930s, a British socialite's tell-all story of her heroin addiction made the astounding claim that Branson had been a spy, recruited by the British Secret Intelligence Service to expose drug-smuggling rings in France. She "had played with the fire of spying," according to this account, before she was discovered and eliminated by the drug lords she had been investigating.

France's "Valley of Hell Mystery," as it came to be known, inspired at least one work of fiction. In 1939, British author E. R. Punshon published *Murder Abroad*, one of a series of mystery novels featuring police investigator Bobby Owen. Punshon moved the crime scene to Auvergne, in central France, and changed the cause of death to drowning in a well, but the victim is a transplanted English artist with an aristocratic background. When the local authorities declare the death a suicide, her family in Britain asks Owen to investigate. Among the murder suspects is the handsome young son of a hotel keeper.

The Branson case had unfolded like the plot of a crime novel, even if it was a story with plenty of loose ends. One newspaper feature described it as "A Thriller from Real Life." The setting was faraway and exotic. The victim and the man suspected of killing her had been secret lovers. In a stranger-than-fiction twist, Branson's death was either a murder staged to look like a suicide, or a suicide staged to look like a murder. And a brilliant detective, Chief Inspector Guibbal, had been parachuted in to identify a suspect and crack the case. But with the only suspect cleared by a jury, it was a story without an ending. There was no justice for the victim and no punishment for the culprit.

Almost a century after her body was found, Branson's murder remains unsolved and unexplained. "The secret of Olive Branson's death will never be known," the *St. Louis Post-Dispatch* correctly predicted in 1929. "The Valley of Hell will hold this dark secret as it has held many others in the past."

A Murder in Beverlywood

Priscilla Scott Rhoades

In the city of Los Angeles, in the 1960s, the zip code 90035 is considered one of the most desirable addresses in all of Southern California. Known as Beverlywood, the fashionable West LA neighborhood is described as "a leafy suburban community" by real estate agents promoting the single-family homes to buyers who can afford the price and will agree to abide by the CC&Rs of the Beverlywood Homes Association. The saying among agents is that if their clients don't qualify to buy into 90210—the zip code of Beverly Hills—but still want the cachet of being close to BH, then Beverlywood is for them.

The Association's Covenants, Conditions, and Restrictions ensure that the planned community maintains a uniformly high-end look of traditional three- or four-bedroom luxury houses, professionally landscaped front yards, private parks, and clean sidewalks shaded by mature trees.

A major selling point is safety. Residents feel secure in the family-friendly community, and for good reason. Beverlywood is the kind of place where you can leave your door unlocked, knowing that the crime rate is close to zero. Bad things don't happen here. Not in Beverlywood.

That's why the brutal murder of sixteen-year-old Stephanie Gorman in her parent's home on Hillsboro Avenue is so shocking. So unbelievable.

That day—Thursday, August 5, 1965—begins like any other weekday that summer. Edward Gorman, a prominent attorney in private practice specializing in estate planning, drives downtown to his office in the historic Commercial Exchange Building at 416 West Eighth Street. With him is the older Gorman girl, nineteen-year-old Cheryl. A junior at the University of California, Los Angeles, Cheryl is living at home for the summer, working in her dad's office between semesters.

Cheryl is not the only daughter earning pocket money. Since she was eleven, Stephanie has been getting bit parts in movies as an extra. Although film work is fun, she doesn't intend to make a career out of Hollywood. She's a bright girl, a high school honor student, getting straight As. She'll go on to college and then decide on a direction for her professional life.

Mrs. Gorman—Julie—has plans to be out of the house that day as well. After a mid-morning tennis date at the nearby Hillcrest Country Club, she has a hair appointment at a beauty salon later in the afternoon.

That morning, Stephanie will attend a summer class at Alexander Hamilton High School, known by its students as "Hami." Located a mile south of Beverlywood on Robertson Boulevard, Hamilton High is a well-regarded public school that brings in students from the affluent neighborhoods of Beverlywood, Cheviot Hills, and Castle Heights, as well as less privileged teenagers from the Pico-Robertson area.

By noon, Stephanie's class is over. It's a warm, sunny day, not too smoggy, and she could walk, but she accepts a ride home with a girlfriend, Ilene Jackman, who also lives on Hillsboro Avenue. With them is another Hami student, Paul Bernstein, a nice Jewish boy Stephanie has dated casually. Ilene drops Paul off first; then a few blocks later, she pulls her Mustang over to the brown stucco and clapboard house at the corner of Hillsboro and Sawyer. She watches Stephanie get out of the car and walk to the back gate. Ilene drives away.

Later, Ilene tells police she thinks the time is about 12:45 p.m. Detectives piece together what they believe happened next.

Stephanie lets herself into the backyard through the closed gate. It's a secluded area, hidden by privacy trees, rose bushes, and shrubs. She's greeted by the family dog, a poodle. She makes sure the gate is latched so the poodle won't get out.

Walking on the flagstone tiles of the patio, she reaches the sliding glass door. Since no one is home, it's locked. She uses her key, goes inside, and then makes a critical decision. At this point she decides either to leave the back door unlocked, knowing that Beverlywood is a safe neighborhood, or to lock it because she's home alone. There is no way to know which choice she made.

The house has three bedrooms: the parents', Cheryl's, and Stephanie's. Stephanie goes to her bedroom and sets her books and purse on a shelf. Then she strolls to the kitchen for something to eat.

The police can only speculate about what happens now. There is no sign of forced entry. This is not a break-in. There are three possibilities. One: the intruder lets himself into the house using the unlocked back door. Two: the back door is locked, so he knocks on the glass, and Stephanie answers. Three: he knocks on the front door, and Stephanie opens it.

No matter which door he uses, the intruder manages to find, talk, or barge his way into the house. Once inside and out of the view of neighbors, he attacks Stephanie, stunning her with an unexpected punch to the face. The blow is so hard it gives her a concussion and knocks her unconscious. The coroner, Dr. Harold Kade, finds swelling, bruising, and deep lacerations on her lips and in her mouth.

Stephanie is wearing jean shorts, a knit top, athletic socks, and tennis shoes. Her assailant drags her to Cheryl's bedroom. Dr. Kade sees "brush burns on the right hip," indicating that Stephanie was pulled across a surface like a rug.

The fact that the attacker chooses Cheryl's bedroom rather than Stephanie's may or may not be significant. Detectives consider the possibility that the older sister was the intended target. The Gorman sisters are only three years apart in age. They look alike and often dress in similar clothes.

The intruder comes to the crime prepared. He brings along a knife, a small caliber semiautomatic gun, and mason line, a type of rope used by landscapers and construction workers. He drops a cord strand near the front door and never bothers to pick it up.

He leaves no fingerprints. Detectives speculate that he wears gloves or, because this is his first offense, he doesn't bother to conceal his hands. In the 1960s, fingerprint analysis still has to be done manually by comparing lifted prints to photographic records of known lawbreakers. It's a time-consuming task, subject to human error. Suspects with no criminal record are not in the system.

With his unconscious victim dragged to Cheryl's room, he uses the mason line to tie Stephanie's wrists to the legs of the bed. He rips off her shorts and underpants, knotting the underwear around her neck. He cuts away her top and bra.

Detectives think that around this time, Stephanie regains consciousness and realizes what's happening to her. She struggles against her restraints, managing to break the cord on her right wrist. She puts up a fierce struggle. She fights for her life.

Her attacker panics. *It wasn't supposed to go down like this.* His psychosexual fantasy isn't playing out the way he had imagined. He remembers the gun. It's possible he hadn't intended to use it. Perhaps it was for show. A threat. But now, this is real.

His heart is racing. In a rush of adrenaline, he fires the gun four times. The bullets hit Stephanie twice in the chest, once in the neck, and once in the head. She dies from a massive hemorrhage.

There's blood everywhere, including the back spatter on him. He finds towels in the master bathroom and wipes off the gore. Is he in shock? Is he disassociating from what he's done? Or is he a remorseless sociopath who has killed before?

There are expelled, Western-brand shell casings on the bloodstained carpet. He doesn't stop to pick them up. He goes through the house and out the sliding glass door into the backyard. He drops the towels on the flagstone patio. He walks out of the gate onto Sawyer Street and disappears forever.

Julie stops at the house after her tennis game. It's 3:00 p.m., later than she had intended. She had planned to be there when Stephanie arrived home from school, but she had been pressured into playing another game by some friends at the country club.

"I was just walking out, but they begged me to fill in so they could play doubles," she tells detectives. That decision will haunt her for the rest of her life. "Why? Why did I stay to play? I didn't even want to. Maybe I could have saved her. Or maybe I would have been killed, instead of Stephanie."

Julie notices that the door to Cheryl's bedroom is closed. That's not unusual. The house is quiet. Nothing seems out of place. She cleans up and heads out to her hair appointment.

Cheryl and Edward arrive home around six o'clock. Cheryl goes to her bedroom. She sees the body first. Her father hears her screaming and hurries to the room. Cheryl rushes past him, away from the house, across the street to a neighbor's home where a doctor lives. The doctor isn't there, but a visiting friend follows her back to the Gorman residence. By this time Edward has called the police, and the Western Division of the LAPD are already there with their yellow tape. This is a crime scene now. The police tell the neighbor's friend to leave. He does.

Julie comes home with newly coiffed hair. She's told that something terrible has happened. She's told to brace herself, then given the horrific, unimaginable news. Her daughter is dead. Stephanie has been murdered.

———

The press coverage starts the next day with the morning edition of the *Los Angeles Times*. "Honor Student. L.A. GIRL SLAIN" the headline shouts in bold face type.

> *A beautiful 16-year-old girl who was an honor student and reportedly had appeared as a dancer in six movies was murdered and sexually assaulted Thursday afternoon in her West Los Angeles home. The nude body was discovered in her bedroom of the $65,000 home at 1929 Hillsboro Avenue by her father, Edward, and a sister, Cheryl, 19.*
>
> *...She had been shot three or four times in the head and chest and she had been choked with an undergarment which was found twisted around her neck. The coroner's office said death was caused by the gunshot wounds.*
>
> *Four .22-caliber shells were found near the body but police were unable to find a murder weapon despite an intensive search of the neighborhood, three blocks east of the Hillcrest Country Club.*

The media try to restrain themselves, but the story is too tempting. The tabloids splash her picture across their covers. Family and friends and complete strangers can read all the salacious details of what the media call "a sex slaying."

The *LA Times* hedges its bets. It's betting Stephanie is a "good girl," so they lead with the honor student honorific. But there may be a darker element, so they mention the connection to Hollywood: an honor student and *reportedly* a dancer in movies. Just in case.

In the 1960s, the press, police, and courts still use an old-boy-network standard for judging the guilt or innocence of young women. A sexual assault victim is considered blameless if she is deemed a good girl and somehow complicit in her victimization if she's not. Stephanie appears to be a good girl—an honor student from an upper-middle-class family living in an upscale neighborhood—but reporters want to dig into her film work before they anoint her. There's that connection to movies. Everyone in LA knows that the entertainment business is not exactly a squeaky-clean industry.

The police investigation continues. Ten LAPD men in total are assigned to the case. Detectives ask Edward and Julie if Stephanie was sexually active. The parents insist she wasn't. So do her sister Cheryl and Stephanie's friends, and also Paul, the boy she dated. Privately, among themselves, the authorities debate her virginity. The family's doctor says Stephanie was a virgin the last time he examined her, in April.

By the time of the autopsy in August, the hymen had been broken. The coroner, Dr. Kade, speculates it may have been ruptured naturally over the summer, through exercise or a nonsexual activity. Stephanie is athletic. She plays tennis at the country club more often than her mother. It could have happened that way.

Dr. Kade finds no evidence of foreign fluids in her vagina or rectum and no lacerations there. The uterus, fallopian tubes, and ovaries are normal, he says. Although police find a semen sample on the bedspread, Dr. Kade does not find one inside the victim. Stephanie wasn't raped.

Her film work turns out to be innocent. She's an extra in a crowd scene showcasing Hayley Mills in Disney's *Pollyanna*. She disappears among a throng of fresh-faced girls watching Ann-Margret sing in *Bye Bye Birdie*. Stephanie is a good girl; everyone agrees.

Friday morning, the principal of Hamilton High School makes a grim announcement. Principal Richard Nida confirms that Stephanie Gorman has been murdered. Nida repeats what he's been told by the police, that Stephanie let the intruder inside her home. Like everyone else, Nida is shocked and brokenhearted about the tragedy. He finishes by telling the students that detectives will be in later to talk to them.

The detectives arrive to interview Stephanie's classmates. Both the girls and the boys are having trouble processing the trauma, but the impact is most noticeable in the girls. For many of them, Stephanie's death will be a turning point in their lives, a dividing line between the *before* of innocence and trust, and the *after* of suspicion and fear.

Investigators check the records of all 3,200 Hamilton High students. They discover arrest records on 250 of the boys for crimes ranging from petty theft and burglary to peeking while loitering and indecent exposure. Those boys are interrogated and cleared.

Hamilton students are stunned by the killing of one of their own. Some of them show up at the Gorman home on Friday evening, just to stand across the street and stare hollow-eyed at the house, wrapped in police tape. *How could this have happened here?*

The police cast a wider net.

———————

"Did you know this girl?" my mother asks me.

It's Saturday, August 7, 1965, and I'm at her apartment near the corner of Pico and La Cienega Boulevard for my weekly visitation. An "unfit mother," she suffers from bipolar disorder—it's obvious in hindsight—but has been misdiagnosed over the years as "depressed," "hysterical," or "schizophrenic." Her meds don't work, and she's prone to periodic breakdowns. I've been placed in foster care and am growing up in a home about a half-mile away.

My mother is holding the morning's *LA Times*. "Police Seek Clues in Sex Slaying of Girl, 16," the headline reads. There's a black-and-white photo of Stephanie.

"No," I say. "She was at Hami. I don't start Hami until January."

My mother has lost track of which grade I'm in. I'm a senior at Louis Pasteur Junior High, a Central LA feeder school for Alexander Hamilton High.

"Awful," she says about Stephanie's death, turning the page, looking for better news.

————————

Detectives follow up on leads. A neighbor's gardener, George Iwasaki, tells police that between one and two in the afternoon on Thursday he noticed a man peering into a bedroom window of the Gorman residence. Iwasaki describes the man as a "Latin type" Caucasian, about forty-three to forty-five years old, approximately five feet, seven inches tall and 140 pounds, with unkempt hair and sallow cheeks needing a shave.

The Peeping Tom was wearing a light-blue cotton twill shirt and trousers that looked like a uniform of some kind. A sketch artist works with Iwasaki to come up with a drawing for release to the press.

Meanwhile, police question everyone—virtually all the kids in Stephanie's social circle, boys whom Cheryl has dated, teachers, school counselors, relatives, members of the Hillcrest Country Club, gardeners past and present, mail carriers, gas meter readers, even appliance repairmen who have serviced homes in the district.

And neighbors.

A neighbor says she heard screaming around 3:30 p.m. to 4:00 p.m., but thought it was the Gorman sisters playing.

Another neighbor mentions finding the Gormans' poodle loose on the street. She returned the dog to the backyard around four o'clock, she says. The gate had been left open.

Several neighbors tell police that young "Negro" kids were selling candy door-to-door. The police track down the boys and clear them.

Other neighbors report seeing two suspicious Black men driving slowly around the neighborhood in a 1955 Ford Fairlane. The men are found and questioned. They were distributing handbills. They're released.

A young man—we'll call him Dave—phones the West LA police station on Friday. He wants them to know that he was at the Gorman house on Thursday, looking for someone who used to live there. He parked his car in the driveway. He just wants them to know that. The police say thank you and file the message along with all the other calls coming in.

The media coverage brings out the crazies, the eccentrics, the sad.

Julie finds something strange lying by the side of the house. It's a child's doll with its head torn off. The police take it into evidence, although they don't think it's connected to this crime.

Cheryl gets threatening phone calls. "You're next," a male voice tells her. She can't wait to move back to Sigma Delta Tau, a Jewish sorority at UCLA. She'll do that in September.

A bartender at the Red Rogue on Melrose Avenue, an establishment owned by Judy Garland, calls in about an odd customer—a White guy who comes in on Thursday morning, August 5. "They don't know what's happening," he tells the bartender. "You'll read all about it in the paper. My time's running out. Everybody thinks I'm a clown." He leaves by taxi, vanishing into the anonymity of the sprawling Southland.

An unemployed cable splicer named Henry—"Henry the Confessor"—calls in to claim the crime. He's arrested and later let go when he admits he had been drinking when he called the tip line. He was lonely and needed someone to talk to, he says.

A suspect matching the Peeping Tom sketch is arrested in Palm Springs. Police grill Buddy Rogers, a homeless man from Louisiana. Buddy has an alibi. Detectives turn him loose.

The LAPD follows up on all leads, waiting for a break in the case. They don't get one. They're still hopeful, but they know that with each passing hour, the chances of solving this crime diminish. In 1965, the clearance rate on murders in the US is good; 90 percent of them are solved. The detectives working the Gorman case don't want Stephanie to be part of the 10 percent that aren't.

Exactly one week after the Gorman murder, on Thursday, August 12, a news story bumps Stephanie from the pages of the *LA Times*. "1,000 RIOT IN L.A." the headline warns. "Routine Arrest of 3 Sparks Watts Melee; 8 Blocks Sealed Off."

The *Times* tells readers that "an estimated 1,000 persons rioted in the Watts district Wednesday night and attacked police and motorists with rocks, bricks and bottles before some 100 officers attempted to quell the five-hour melee...."

The uprising lasts six days, escalating into the most violent confrontation between police and Black people in the city's history to that date. Before it's over, fourteen thousand National Guard troops have been brought in to assist the police in putting down the rebellion. In the end, thirty-four people are dead, and LA has suffered forty million dollars in property damage.

In the aftermath, Angelenos debate the causes of the riots. Ultraconservatives believe that radical influences, including secret Communist agents, are agitating "Negroes" in the slums. White liberals point to the problems inherent in systemic racism, especially the role of residential segregation in oppressing Black citizens. There are letters to the editor printed in the *LA Times* and the *LA Herald Examiner*. There are opinion pieces and follow-up articles. TV newscasters play the same inflammatory footage over and over.

The Watts riots throw a monkey wrench into the gears of the Gorman investigation. The police lose more than a week while their attention is turned to the crisis at hand. The media, too, forget about Stephanie; she's old news.

By the time the riots are quelled and the fires extinguished, Stephanie's murder inquiry has stalled. Unable to solve the case using local resources, on August 22, the LAPD issues a nationwide bulletin with a suspect sketch of the man identified by Iwasaki. The *LA Times* publishes the drawing with a short article, but it's on page nine. Stephanie is no longer of front-page interest.

By the end of August, the *LA Times* mentions the Gorman case only briefly, on page twenty-six, next to a two-third-page ad for "Thrifty's 29¢ Infant's Training Pants." The newspaper erroneously reports that Stephanie was raped during her assault.

In 1965, the US has a homicide rate that is approximately five times higher than other Western nations. In that year, there are 9,960 murders in the country. In the state of California alone, there are 880 homicides. In response to the nationwide bulletin issued by the LAPD, responses pour in from police stations around the country on countless perpetrators with similar MOs. Each perpetrator is considered and investigated. Everyone is eliminated. Nothing pans out. There are no matches to the prints found at the crime scene and no matches to the gun used in the murder.

The year 1965 comes to an end. It's January 1966 by the time the crime lab results are returned on the blood and semen samples taken from the bedroom and the towels left on the patio. The blood is determined to be type O. That's Stephanie's blood type. It's probably her blood, but it could be the killer's. The semen stain from the bedspread is inconclusive and could match A or O blood type.

A hair is identified that doesn't belong to anyone in the Gorman home. It's Caucasian. In all likelihood, the killer is White.

The police remember a caller from last August, a young man who said he had driven to the Gorman house on the day of the murder. They track him down and bring him in for questioning. Dave is a twenty-one-year-old white guy, a local boy. Off the record, police describe him as "bizarre-looking. Longhaired and kind of crazy-looking."

Dave repeats his story. He tells detectives he was looking for his friend Bob, thinking he still lived in that house at the corner of Hillsboro and Sawyer.

Dave says, "It was about two or three in the afternoon. I pulled into the driveway and honked the horn. No one came out, so I left. I thought

I saw someone peeking out of the window. I called police because I thought I might have some information that might help them."

Detectives follow up with Bob, who casts doubt on Dave's story. Bob says Dave *knows* where he lives; he's got his current address. Bob says his family *used* to live there, but they sold the Hillsboro house years ago to the Gormans. Dave knew that. Bob doesn't know why Dave would have gone to that house if he was looking for him.

The police talk to Dave's mother and brother. His brother says, "I don't know why you want to talk to him. He told me that he was at the Gorman house two hours before it happened."

The detectives think this is odd. How does Dave know what time the murder happened? Even the police are unsure, guessing it was probably sometime between one and three in the afternoon—around the time Dave said he showed up—although it's possible it could have been slightly later. A neighbor says she heard what she thought was the Gorman sisters screaming in play between 3:30 p.m. and 4:00 p.m. But she could have been wrong about the time.

The police bring Dave back in for more questioning. As it turns out, Dave is a Hami High alumnus. It seems that when Dave was a senior at Hamilton High, Cheryl Gorman was a freshman. Maybe that's the connection—Cheryl. Not Stephanie, who didn't arrive at Hami until after Dave was gone.

They check out Dave's criminal record. He's got an outstanding warrant in Orange County for a bounced check. It's something, but not particularly pertinent. But then they notice the other charge. There's a Penal Code 288 in his past for lewd conduct. When he was a juvenile, Dave was arrested for a "lewd or lascivious act with a child under the age of fourteen." Now, *that's* something.

They ask him to take a polygraph test. Dave refuses; in fact, he leaves the interview. But then he changes his mind; he calls back, saying he's ready to take the test now. The police schedule the polygraph, but at the last minute, Dave calls again and cancels. In lieu of the test, the detectives ask him to sign a written statement, verifying what he's told them. Dave refuses.

That's it. The police obtain an arrest warrant and book him for first-degree murder. After two days in jail, Dave agrees to that polygraph test. The detectives are hopeful. But...

Dave passes the poly. His prints don't match any of the hundreds found at the crime scene. He doesn't own a gun. The police put him in a line-up in front of Iwasaki. The gardener says no, not that one. "He isn't the man I saw at the window."

There's no reason to hold Dave. The police have to let him go.

They're back to nowhere.

————

It's January 1966. I start my freshman semester at Alexander Hamilton High School. Stephanie's classmates are still in mourning, some of the girls suffering from what we now recognize as post-traumatic stress disorder. They're afraid of strangers and mistrustful of nearly everyone else. In their parents' Beverlywood and Cheviot Hills and Castle Heights homes, they double-check that doors are locked and curtains are drawn.

They're juniors now, a class ahead of me in school. I don't know them. Hamilton High is socially stratified; even by the usual high school standards, it's exceptionally cliquish and snobby. Kids from Beverlywood don't associate with kids from Pico-Robertson. Jewish kids party with Jewish kids, Black kids with Black kids. Minority *shiksas* like me socialize with anybody who accepts them.

I hang loosely with the hippies, the misfits at Hami who smoke dope and drop acid and hitchhike down Sunset Boulevard. My girlfriends and I date older guys we meet on the Strip. We're lucky. Nothing very bad ever happens to us during those years, despite all the risks we take.

In 1966, the media stop following the Stephanie Gorman murder.
The police are frustrated. They've gone through five thousand names,
compared the fingerprints of one thousand sex offenders to the prints
lifted from the crime scene, examined more than two hundred arrest
records, followed up on sixty obscene phone call reports, and consulted
with police departments across the country. They've lifted every dirty
rock in LA to see what kind of lowlife is hiding underneath. They've
turned up nothing, gotten nowhere.

There are active crimes that have a better chance of being solved.
The detectives are told to focus on those. The sixteen boxes of files and
evidence on the Gorman case are shelved.

It's cold in LA.

_____

Like so many couples who experience the tragic death of a child, the
Gormans' marriage falls apart. In 1969, after twenty-four years together,
they divorce. Julie remarries and tries to move on with her life. Edward
does the same. His law career advances, and in 1983 he becomes a
Superior Court judge in Los Angeles. At the same time, his health begins
to decline. For many years he's suffered from heart problems. In 1987, he
dies, quite literally, of a broken heart. He's buried in Hillside Memorial
Park in Culver City, next to Stephanie, "beloved daughter and sister who
touched the hearts of all who knew her."

Cheryl graduates from UCLA and becomes a psychologist with
a practice in West LA. She's a good therapist; she has empathy and
can relate to clients who have suffered trauma. Cheryl marries and has
one child.

In 2000, Cheryl is at a party. She's a mature woman now, with a
grown child. A friend is there with her date, an LAPD detective named

Mike Mejia. Cheryl mentions to Detective Mejia that her sister Stephanie was murdered many years ago. The case was never solved.

Detective Mejia is interested. Give him the information, and he'll look into it, he says.

He does. Mejia searches the city's archives, finds the boxes of Stephanie Gorman files, and consults his supervisor, who agrees the murder is worth reopening. They both know that advances in technology using DNA analysis and automated fingerprint searches have solved cold cases like this one. But this case is old and complex, the supervisor says; it needs a specialist. He passes it along to Detective Dave Lambkin, supervisor of the Rape Special Section, the division that handles sex crimes.

Lambkin brings in his partner Detective Tim Marcia, and together they consult with Mejia as they go through the boxes. Lambkin knows that DNA is the key to solving this kind of crime. Unfortunately, he soon learns that through a combination of computer and human error, a "disposition card" was issued on the Gorman case in 1989, giving the supervisor in charge of storage the option of disposing of the evidence. Normally, destruction of evidence doesn't happen until a case has been cleared. Evidence involving a homicide, particularly an unsolved homicide, is *never* to be destroyed.

But in 1989, because the warehouse was overcrowded, that supervisor scanned the disposition card and authorized the destruction of evidence taken from the Gorman crime scene. Lambkin wants to know what disciplinary action was taken against him. He's outraged to hear there was none. Mejia says he spoke to the man, who had retired from the force. The retired supervisor said he didn't remember the Gorman case; he didn't remember authorizing the destruction of that evidence.

Now, in 2000, Lambkin reads the original police notes about Dave, the Hamilton High alumnus who told detectives he parked in the driveway on the afternoon of the murder. If the DNA evidence hadn't been destroyed in 1989, if that bedspread with the semen stain had not been trashed, Dave could have been brought in for one last questioning. Dave's DNA could have been checked against the bedspread evidence and his innocence—or guilt—confirmed. That's not possible now.

Marcia uncovers more information about Dave. It seems he's been in additional trouble since the Gorman case. In 1966, after the West LAPD release him from the first-degree murder charge that doesn't stick, they notify Orange County police, who promptly arrest Dave on his bad check warrant.

In 1986, Dave is arrested again, this time for prostitution after offering his services to an undercover female officer.

"What do I get for seventy-five bucks?" she asks.

"Are you into spanking, fetishes, or bondage?"

"No, I'm just a normal person."

"Then I'll give you straight sexual intercourse," he says.

Dave waives his rights, admitting that he's a male prostitute for women. Not only that, he tells police, "I've got four whores working for me."

Marcia finds another arrest record on him, this one for spousal abuse.

"Yeah, I hit her," Dave confesses, rationalizing that it's his wife's fault. "She's banging everyone in the building."

Lambkin is angry and frustrated. He and Marcia think Dave is their number-one suspect, but there's nothing they can do without DNA evidence.

Just as frustrating is the fact that a number of important files are missing from the Gorman crime boxes. The handwritten statements from the original interviews are gone, leaving only assorted notes and synopses.

The only good news is that the fingerprints are still there. That's all he and Marcia have to go on.

———

They run the fingerprints through a database that wasn't around in the 1960s, and they get a hit. There's one fingerprint that doesn't belong at the crime scene. That fingerprint doesn't match any of the family members or anyone else who had a legitimate reason to be in the house. Once again, Lambkin finds reason to be hopeful.

But not for long. The fingerprint belongs to a friend of a doctor who lived across the street from the Gormans. Lambkin finds the friend still living in LA. He cooperates fully, explaining what happened that day. He says the older Gorman girl ran over to the doctor's house, extremely upset, saying something about her sister being shot. The friend followed her back to her house and went inside with the girl. The police were there, and they told him to leave. He did. That's why his fingerprints were at the crime scene.

The friend tells Lambkin he was surprised he wasn't questioned back in 1965, but no one talked to him then. Lambkin is deflated. More human error. Police are supposed to "secure the witnesses" by identifying everyone at a crime scene so they can be contacted later. No one thought to ask the friend his name.

"If the patrol officer had identified him, it would have saved us months of work," Marcia says.

That was their last hope. They've reached a dead end. There's nothing more they can do. Barring a death-bed confession, the case is over.

———————

But not quite. LAPD Detective Rick Jackson gets bored being retired. It's hard to let go of crime-solving after twenty years on the force, after two decades of living 24/7 trying to catch killers. It gets into your blood.

In the mid-1990s, Jackson starts working with writers like James Ellroy, Joseph Wambaugh, and Michael Connelly. Those writers go on to become bestselling authors, reaching audiences in the millions. Sometimes the stories they write result in a cold case getting solved.

Maybe it will happen again. In 2002, Jackson tells James Ellroy about the Stephanie Gorman case. He shows Ellroy the files, the police notes, the photographs. Ellroy is sickened by what he sees. He went to Fairfax High School, not far from Hamilton High. He knew girls like Stephanie. This feels personal.

He writes the story for *Gentleman's Quarterly*. It's published in the January 2003 issue, is well-received, and earns a place in the annual *Best American Crime Writing* anthology, with an introduction by Joseph Wambaugh.

Unfortunately, Ellroy's article contributes nothing toward solving the crime. There are no more tips, no more witness statements, no new information.

Stephanie has been dead for thirty-eight years.

"It's over. It's not over," Ellroy writes. "Closure is nonsense. Nothing this bad ever ends."

———

In 2004, Julie tells Detective Lambkin that she tries not to think about the murder of her daughter, but when she does, she remains unconvinced that it was a stranger who assaulted Stephanie that horrible day in August 1965. What if Stephanie opened the door to her killer? Invited him inside because she thought she had nothing to fear?

After the murder, "I kept looking at everyone," Julie says. "I've always worried it was someone we knew."

———

Julie passes away in 2013. Like Edward and Stephanie, Julie is buried in Hillside Memorial Park.

Of the four family members living in the Gorman home in 1965, only Cheryl is still alive today.

———

In November 1965, a ballot measure is brought before the members of the Beverlywood Homes Association. The association's president, Robert Schwartz, wants to hire a private security firm to patrol the neighborhood. That would require an assessment of approximately $24,000 a year, to be divided equally among the 1,342 homeowners.

Although it fails to garner enough votes to pass in November, in December it's voted on again. Homeowners have had more time to think about how much they're willing to sacrifice to protect their neighborhood. This time the measure receives the 75 percent affirmative ballot it requires to be approved.

Schwartz tells a reporter for the *LA Times* that the police are "doing a good job under the circumstances." But after Stephanie Gorman's murder last August, residents feel that additional security is needed before they can feel safe again in Beverlywood.

"The crime occurred," he says, "and it could happen again. My kids could be next."

———

To date, the murder of Stephanie Gorman remains unsolved.

The Enduring Mystery of Julia Wallace

Cathy Pickens

Why do some crimes, whether solved or unsolved, stick with us, while others drift away from our collective memory, no matter the drama or outrage at the time? The 1931 murder of homemaker Julia Wallace in the cozy front room of her Liverpool home was, on the surface, a rather ordinary domestic case, one that should receive an ordinary explanation and fade away.

Except that it didn't.

The very un-ordinariness of the murder of Julia Wallace is what has captivated famous crime novelists and journalists and do-it-yourself sleuths for almost a hundred years.

The Wallaces

The main events took place in Liverpool, England, on the Monday and Tuesday evenings of January 19 and 20, 1931. William Herbert Wallace (fifty-two), employed as one of the respectable, reliable door-to-door agents for the Prudential Assurance Company, headed out for an evening with his Liverpool Central Chess Club, which met twice weekly at Cottle's City Café near the River Mersey. Wallace had been a member for about eight years but only attended once a week, at most.

His job required that he make calls to collect from his policy holders, so he had missed matches recently, either for work or because he and his wife were just recovering from bouts with the flu.

Wallace and his wife Julia lived at 29 Wolverton Street, a terraced house in the Anfield neighborhood, for sixteen of their eighteen married years. The couple had no children and, to all appearances, were quiet, gentle, and devoted to each other. Julia cared for William during chronic kidney bouts. Their nearest neighbors in their attached housing never heard so much as a quarrel from the couple. They were not the kind to attract police attention or make headlines.

A much-reprinted photo of Julia shows a woman with thick, soft hair under a brimmed hat, a smooth, slender face with a slight smile and a dreamy gaze. Accounts vary as to her age, but their shared tombstone gives it as two years younger than William. He was tall and thin, with wire-rimmed glasses and a brushy mustache, and always shown wearing a vested suit. He looked older than his fifty-two years, possibly because of that chronic kidney ailment, and could've passed for a professor or a scholarly cleric, gentle and bookish.

William sometimes lectured in chemistry at the local technical school and liked to indulge in amateur chemistry and electronics experiments in his home laboratory. The couple often played music together in the evening, he on the violin and she on the piano. He was described as somewhat shy, but interesting once he came out of his shell. In later years, the stories painted him as a better chess player than he was in life, perhaps because a genius chess player makes for a more chillingly credible criminal mastermind than a mediocre chess player does.

In later retellings, the contrasts defined this story. Was the couple quiet and engaged in their gentle, studious pastimes? Or too locked away and too secretive? Was William shy? Or cold and hard? Were they in love? Or had he tired of Julia in ways that only make sense from inside a marriage?

The Chess Club

On that January Monday evening, William said later he hesitated to leave his wife. As they recovered from a flu, hers had settled into a troublesome bronchitis, but he felt fine and she encouraged him to go ahead with his outing.

Wallace arrived at the chess club meeting soon after 7:30 p.m. The matches were scheduled in advance, and lack of punctuality was penalized. Captain Samuel Beattie, who always came early on club nights to set up for the evening's matches, passed along a message for Wallace. Someone had phoned before he arrived, asking for him. A Mr. R. M. Qualtrough wanted him to call at 25 Menlove Gardens East the next evening at 7:30. Qualtrough was too busy to call back to speak to Wallace personally. "Oh, no, I can't, I'm too busy. I've got my girl's twenty-first birthday party on, and I want to see Mr. Wallace on a matter of business. It's something in the nature of his business."

Captain Beattie's recall of that conversation became critical, given the events of the following night. Beattie had the caller carefully repeat the message so he could be certain of the details, and Wallace later copied it into his pocket notebook. Wallace wasn't sure where Menlove Gardens East was located. Neither were the other players he asked. But he was confident he could find it. After all, successful insurance agents weren't known for letting sales slip away from them just because they had to travel a bit and ask for directions, especially in the midst of the Depression.

After the chess match, Wallace walked outside with friends, elated and recounting the final moves of his win of the night. Contrary to later reports, while Wallace loved to play chess, he wasn't a chess genius, so he was enjoying his win. The group broke up outside and he returned home, the end of an ordinary evening.

In retrospect, of course, each detail would be rehashed and recalibrated over the coming decades. Perfectly ordinary things, like leaving a message for a man at a restaurant where he was known to play chess, would become suspicious. But at the end of Monday, things were still ordinary, predictable, even mundane.

The Search for Qualtrough

On Tuesday evening, as with any good Golden Age detective novel, pinning down exact times became central to piecing together the story. Every second would be examined and dissected and reassembled, even casual and oft-repeated actions that are difficult to remember accurately because they happen too routinely. The most reliable evidence says the milk delivery boy saw Julia between 6:30 and 6:45 p.m. when he came to the door to drop off their order and collect the empty bottles.

The latest time Wallace could have left the house was 6:50 p.m. since the next independent sighting of him was at 7:06, when he transferred streetcars two miles from his home. The tram schedules also make 6:50 the most likely departure time for him to be on his way to meet his new client at 7:30 in Menlove Gardens East. Conductors and a constable later remembered Wallace because of all his questions about where to transfer on his three-tram ride and where he could find the address. He had a ten-minute ride before another transfer at Penny Lane. Then, about seven blocks later, he disembarked at Menlove Avenue.

What followed was a runabout game of frustration for a man anxious to keep an appointment. Who would've thought Liverpool had a Menlove Gardens North, South, and West, but no such Menlove Gardens East? He asked a passerby. He asked a constable. He stopped by the newsagent's and checked a directory. He rang the bell at Menlove Gardens West, but they knew no R. M. Qualtrough.

The Discovery

At some point, Wallace gave up the quest. By 8:45 p.m., he was at his front door, facing another challenge. His key wouldn't work. He knocked, but there was no answer. He circled around to the back of the attached houses and tried that door, finding it also bolted. He tried the front door again, then returned to the back gate.

His neighbors, John and Florence Johnston, stepped out their door as he came once again to try the back door. He asked if they'd heard anything and said Julia couldn't be out because she "has such a bad cold." The Johnstons offered to let him try their key. They had a spare to the Wallaces' house so they could check on the family cat, when needed. This time, though, his key worked. Sometimes the lock did stick.

The neighbors waited for a couple of minutes while Wallace went inside to check the house. They could hear him moving through to the stairs and saw an upstairs bedroom lamp turned brighter. He called out for Julia, then came back downstairs toward the front parlor, the last place he would expect her to be.

He struck a match at the doorway. The Wallaces typically spent most of their time in their combination sitting room and kitchen at the back of the house. Crime scene photos show a room with a large fireplace stove, walls of books, papers scattered on a small desktop, and a dining table with newspapers, scissors, cups, and plates—the evidence of daily life. In this room, they ate their meals and read, and Mr. Wallace did paperwork; he even kept the cash box high on the bookcase, where he placed his daily cash receipts.

The Wallaces rarely used the front parlor except to entertain guests and to play music, so he understandably didn't expect to find his wife in the parlor.

He certainly didn't expect to find her on the floor in front of the unlit fire. Crossing the room, he bent over to light the gas jet, as was their custom when using the room. People are creatures of habit, but as with everything else that happened during these two days, this action would be questioned and doubted. Why not light the lamp closest to the door first? His simple answer—*because we always light the gas first*—wasn't a satisfactory answer for those with raised eyebrows.

He thought perhaps Julia had passed out or had a fit. He hadn't expected to find her with her skull bashed open and blood spattered on the wallpaper. He wouldn't have expected such a scene—unless, as the prosecutor later argued, he'd killed her before he left to look for the phantom Qualtrough. When the gas lit the room, he could see just how bad it was. Or was he seeing again his own handiwork?

Wallace came down the hall to summon the Johnstons, obviously anxious despite his usual stoic demeanor. "Come and see! She's been killed!"

Johnston went for a doctor, though that seemed of little use, and for the police. A search showed the cash box had been robbed, though the takings were scant: only about four pounds missing. He'd made several payouts that week on insurance claims, so the cash receipts were smaller than usual. About five pounds was upstairs, undisturbed.

While Florence Johnston and Wallace waited for authorities, they returned to the front parlor where Julia lay. Florence noticed a Mackintosh stuffed partially under her body—Wallace's Mackintosh, which he'd worn on his morning rounds because of the bad weather and which he'd hung in the front hall when he came home for lunch.

The Mackintosh had been burned, though it hadn't caught fire, and was bloody. But what was it doing under his wife's body? This would become another source of debate. The most creative explanation became a key part of the prosecutor's case.

The Trial

For William Wallace, part of the risk of being a pleasant man in a comfortable marriage with a good job and no known enemies was that, when your wife is killed, you're the only possible suspect.

The prosecution began building its case. The call that summoned Wallace on the snipe hunt for nonexistent Menlove Gardens East came from a call box located about four blocks from the Wallace house, at the intersection he'd passed on his way to play chess the night before the murder. He could've made the call and still gotten to the café just after 7:30.

On the other hand, someone could've watched him leave the house and made the call when the coast was clear, setting up the events for the following night.

Timing proved a problem for the police case, but not an insurmountable one. Julia Wallace was seen, by the most conservative report, at 6:40 on Tuesday evening. Wallace was seen on a tram at 7:06, and he would've had to leave home no later than 6:50. How could he possibly have struck his wife brutally and with such a mess of cast-off blood within that ten-minute timetable? Even if the milk boy saw her as early as 6:30, twenty minutes is a tight fit for such a crime.

Trying to look back in time and analyze the crime scene, especially the blood spatter in the parlor and a blood drop in the upstairs bath, is difficult. With modern forensic techniques—and especially the exaggerations seen regularly on television crime dramas—we expect the scene to reveal more than it reasonably could have in 1931.

Enter the prosecution's Mackintosh theory: in order to quickly kill his wife and protect himself from the blood, Wallace pulled his Mackintosh over his nude body, entered the parlor, did the deed, stuffed the coat under her (after apparently wasting some time trying to burn it in the gas fire), then dressed and left for Menlove Gardens, all in a matter of moments.

A naked murderer—the tabloids loved it. But was it believable? The crime scene was bloody, the wounds were horrible, and the crime would have taken physical and emotional effort. Yet no one saw any signs in Wallace later that evening? Wasn't it also possible Julia had gotten the Mackintosh off the peg and draped it over her shoulders in order to answer a knock at the door and unknowingly admitted her killer?

Of his search for Qualtrough's house, some commented that perhaps Wallace was trying too hard to be noticed, to establish his alibi, to be seen and noted by reliable witnesses. Then again, he was a meticulous, punctual man. That was practically the definition of being a "man from the Pru." And wouldn't he give some outward sign? If not a missed spot of blood on his clothes or in his hair, then a shaking hand or a quaver in his voice, if he'd just beaten his wife in a flurry of eleven vicious blows?

The most likely murder weapon, the fireplace poker, was missing. Why would a murderer risk taking away a murder weapon that belonged in the house? Whether it was Wallace or some mysterious attacker, why not wipe it clean of fingerprints and leave it on the rug? A poker isn't easy to carry away. And if, in keeping with the Mackintosh theory of the murder, Wallace had taken pains to avoid any bloodstains on his person, why then carry a bloody poker out the door? Despite an extensive search of likely hiding spots, the poker was never found.

In the decades that followed, the more people debated the twists in the case, the wilder the theories of motive and execution of the crime became. Close dissection of times and corroborating witnesses leave Wallace almost no time to commit the murder (unless he dressed up as Julia for the benefit of the milk boy—but he was a great deal too tall, among other difficulties with that theory). So some posit the possibility of an accomplice in the crime.

As to motive, neither Wallace nor Julia had an extramarital lover. The police searched diligently and found no whisper of scandal or infidelity, no money troubles, only twenty pounds in life insurance on Julia.

None of those theories offer an explanation as to why Wallace might have wanted his wife dead or, more importantly, why someone would help him and keep quiet for all those years without a hint to anyone. Like most of us, criminals have a hard time not talking about highly emotional or life-changing events, so most talk about their crimes to someone, eventually. Never a breath.

Is part of the lure of this case the buried fear that this could actually happen? That anyone could return home at night, find a loved one dead in a horrible heap on the parlor rug, and find themself hauled into jail, accused, and set for trial? Even if one doesn't identify with mild, bookish William Herbert Wallace, one can identify with heartbreak overlaid with fear, the wordless shock of not being believed.

Fortunately for Wallace, the judge believed him, and did what British judges are allowed to do in summing up the case for the jury. In the US, the law is the judge's purview, while the facts are left for the jury to determine. Unlike in the US, where judges "instruct" jurors on the law they must apply in a case and leave them to apply that law, in British courts the wigged judges give a "summation" of both law and facts before the jury retires to deliberate.

In Wallace's case, presiding judge Mr. Justice Wright was balanced in his summation of the evidence but, according to those who heard not just his words but his tone, he left no doubt how he saw the case and that an acquittal would be proper. But for the jury and other court-watchers, Wallace was not their picture of a grieving husband.

Crime writer F. Tennyson Jesse, who observed the trial, understood why the jury found him guilty after watching his testimony. "People of unpleasing personality," she wrote, "should be advised never to go into the witness box. The jury did not like the man or his manner, which could have been either stoicism or callousness. They did not understand his lack of expression of any kind, and they knew it hid something. It could have hidden sorrow or guilt and they made their choice."

The trial, which began only three months after the murder, lasted four days. The jury deliberated just over an hour before returning a verdict of guilty. Many in the courtroom gasped. In England at the time, guilt meant a mandatory death sentence.

When asked by the judge if he had anything to say, Wallace said only, "I am not guilty. I cannot say anything else."

Judicial time moved quickly in those days. The judge donned the black cap and pronounced his execution date for the following month.

Instead of an execution, though, Britain witnessed a precedent-setting move by the Court of Criminal Appeal, created by the 1907 Criminal Appeal Act. Prior to the Wallace case, its decisions addressed errors by trial judges. In this case, the court overturned the jury's error. The appellate decision found the case had not been proved "with that certainty which is necessary in order to justify a verdict of guilty" and "quashed" the conviction. William Herbert Wallace was a free man.

He got his job back at the Prudential, but a combination of public sentiment that a murderer had walked free and his own increasingly poor health forced Wallace into an in-office job. An accused man could understandably encounter trouble when calling door to door in the city where he'd stood trial. He moved a few miles from Wolverton Street to a cottage in Merseyside, but lived only two years, dying of the kidney ailment that had plagued him for years.

The trial and the appeal did little to settle the case. Who would kill Julia Wallace? If Wallace didn't do it, who did?

One recurring name surfaced very soon after the murder. Wallace had mentioned, in his interview with police, a work colleague with whom he'd had problems—a young man who'd dipped into the company till. The young man—whose father was well-to-do and influential—was later quietly "separated" from the company. Wallace told police he didn't report the thief to the company, but perhaps the young man suspected him nonetheless and held a grudge against Wallace.

The Amateur Detectives

In 1969, British crime historian Jonathan Goodman dug into the resources available at the time and published *The Killing of Julia Wallace*, one of the most cited book-length explorations of the case. In it, he pointed to "Mr. X," the unnamed young man, as the most likely murderer.

In 1981, a year after Mr. X died, British journalist and crime writer Roger Wilkes named him publicly: Richard Gordon Parry. Parry knew Julia and her husband. He'd been to their house. He knew Wallace's routine of storing the day's receipts in a box on the bookshelf. He was a young man with expensive tastes and too little income. He may have blamed Wallace for the loss of his job. He reportedly made a condemning statement on the night of the murder to a garage attendant who found a bloody glove in his car: "If the police found that, it would hang me!"

Given these revelations and discussions, Parry's name has remained a constant in the case debates. Despite his possible alibi, some hypothesize he masterminded the phone call as a distraction for the burglary and that his accomplice murdered Julia when he found her at home.

The debate and attempts at solutions continue today. On January 20, 2021, the ninetieth anniversary of the day of the murder, Mark Russell published *Checkmate: The Wallace Murder Mystery*. Knowledgeable reviewers pronounce it one of the most thoroughly researched and readable accounts. As an interesting sidenote, Russell's grandparents knew the Wallaces and were William's Prudential clients.

At least one online group closed discussion threads because comments got too heated. Another online group investigated and discussed the case, then voted, as a jury would. The majority (62 percent) believed Wallace innocent, that either Parry or his accomplice murdered Julia; but a healthy percentage (37 percent) believed Wallace or his accomplice did it. One percent voted for the "Wallace did it after a coincidental prank call" solution.

Those interested enough in the case to write about it, online and in print, have ranged from writers of traditional British mysteries to at least one American hardboiled crime writer to a British film critic, hardcore chess players, and a variety of crime historians and amateur detectives. Gathering up the myriad discussions and solutions of the case written by those amateur detectives, and totting up those who would vote to condemn Wallace and those who would acquit him, would be an interesting but almost impossible exercise.

Raymond Chandler made notes in his journal about real-life crimes he found interesting. Of this case, he noted, "There is a lot of magoozlum about blood splashes, but we end up with a very vague idea about how much and how far." He felt that, had the police and medical investigation been more meticulous, "there wouldn't have been any chance of Wallace getting away with it, if he was guilty, or of being arrested and tried if he was innocent." The mental effort of committing murder got Chandler's attention as much as the physical evidence: "the judge was the only one to point out that a man may plan a murder very coolly and yet lose his head in the execution of it. But this man got his head back again awfully damn quick…."

Elements of this case can be found in novels by some of the best crime fiction writers of the twentieth century: Christiana Brand had an anonymous caller summon a doctor away from his house in *London Particular* (1952). Agatha Christie refers to the case in a couple of her novels. In *Evil Under the Sun* (1941), she had a character who echoed what observers said about Wallace's appearance in the dock: "He's not the kind that shows anything. That sort makes a bad impression in the witness-box, and yet it's a bit unfair on them really. Sometimes they're as cut up as anything and yet can't show it. That kind of manner made the jury bring in a verdict of guilty against Wallace. It wasn't the evidence. They just couldn't believe that a man could lose his wife and talk and act so coolly about it."

Rather than use the case as fodder for fiction, some detective novelists wrote critical analyses of the case. One of the most widely cited is Dorothy L. Sayers's essay, one of eight essays exploring real murder cases discussed by members of Britain's exclusive Detection Club in *The Anatomy of Murder* (1936). As a plotter of intricate whodunits, Sayers wished the police reports had more detail about the door locks and their functioning, and she also drew the chess connection: the "Wallace murder had no key-move and ended, in fact, in stalemate."

In 2013, in *The Sunday Times*, British mystery novelist P. D. James compared the case to Jack the Ripper "in the amount of writing, both fiction and nonfiction, which it has created." Her theory made international headlines when she said the case was misunderstood simply because no one could believe in a coincidence, that Parry would place a prank call luring Wallace to a nonexistent sales call and Wallace would use that same night to bludgeon his wife to death. Approaching it more as a detective novelist than a detective, she was firmly in the "he did it" camp.

Some approach the case with the attitude of James Agate, British theater critic, as a puzzle worthy of endless debate. He would invite crime historian Edgar Lustgarten to his house: "Come over, my dear boy; let's have a good talk about Wallace." Those talks could carry on into the early-morning hours.

Agate wrote in his published journal, "The Wallace case…was planned with extreme care and extraordinary imagination. Either the murderer was Wallace or it wasn't. If it wasn't, then here at last is the perfect murder. If it was, then here is a murder so nearly perfect that the Court of Criminal Appeal…decided to quash Wallace's conviction."

Lustgarten, in one of their many discussions, asked Agate, "I wonder if he reads the stuff that's written on the crime and sometimes talks about the case among his friends."

"That," said Agate somberly, "is the most shocking thought of all."

For writers and readers of crime fiction, the details over the timetables and the alibi and the door locks and the assumed genius of a chess player were akin to what one might find on the pages of a Golden Age mystery. Wallace's alleged chess prowess seemed to be a particular favorite in tabloid accounts, casting Wallace as a criminal genius who could puzzle one step ahead of the police. Of course, chess aficionados joined crime novelists in a continued dissection of the case.

One reading of the myriad details could point to Wallace's guilt, for who else but a husband—always the first of suspects—would need such elaborate planning for a murder? Another reading turns from the tedious details of when the call came to the chess club and whether one could reasonably assume Wallace would appear at the club that Monday, given his sporadic attention, and instead turned to the characters and the psychology of the puzzle. Could a man who'd never shown a violent tendency or any frustration with his wife brutally batter in her head, leave the house, and win his chess match? Was it really so odd that he wandered around asking questions to confirm the time and the possible location of Menlove Gardens East in such meticulous detail, given his personality?

Was it plausible that a workplace embarrassment could make someone angry enough to plot such a crime? Was the plot hatched simply for robbery, on a night when the burglar expected the insurance box to be full? Was framing the husband for murder part of the plan all along? Or does that just carry the speculation, once again, to too great an extreme?

Edgar Lustgarten gave Julia's murder and its endless questions and fascination an apt summation: other cases, he said, had "more psychological interest, wider human appeal, greater social significance. But, as a mental exercise, as a challenge to one's powers of deduction and analysis, the Wallace murder is in a class by itself. It has all the maddening, frustrating fascination of a chess problem that ends in perpetual check." Each element can point equally to guilt and innocence, he said. "It is preeminently the case where everything is canceled out by something else."

––––––––––

Author's note: If you enjoy digging into details, the trial transcript, investigative notes, and photos are available online. See Wyndham-Brown's trial report reprinted on the Internet Archive, along with The Julia Wallace Murder Foundation website.

A Mystery Within the Vatican's Walls

Deirdre Pirro

If you happened to meet her today, and if what happened to her had never happened, she would probably be an attractive, dark-haired woman of fifty-three, an accomplished, even professional musician, more than likely happily married with a brood of children and surrounded by a large, loving family of siblings, nieces, and nephews. But something *did* happen to her on a busy city street in Rome on June 22, 1983. She disappeared.

Then a vivacious and gregarious teenager of fifteen, Emanuela Orlandi was on her way home from a lesson at the music school in Sant'Apollinare, not far from the Palazzo Madama, the home of the Senate of the Republic of Italy. A talented and passionate musician, she had been studying the piano, side-blown flute, choral singing, and solmization there for several years. She had arrived for her lesson at about four in the afternoon and left ten minutes earlier than usual, at 6:45 p.m. Once outside, she called Federica, one of her three sisters, from a telephone booth to say she was running late because the bus was behind schedule. She also mentioned that a man had stopped her on the street and told her she could get some part-time work during the fashion parade season by handing out pamphlets advertising cosmetics for one of the fashion houses. Her sister warned her against taking up such a proposal until she got home and could talk it over with their mother. This was the last contact Emanuela had with her family.

It later emerged that the cosmetic company mentioned by the stranger had never made any such offer of temporary work, and that the same man had attempted to lure several other young teenage girls with this trap. Nonetheless, a year after Emanuela vanished, another teenage girl in Rome was cajoled into prostitution by a young, self-styled cosmetics company representative, though he proved to have nothing to do with the Orlandi case.

After making the phone call, Emanuela joined two of her classmates from the music school, Maria Grazia and Raffaella, to wait for the bus at another stop in Corso Rinascimento. One after the other, her two friends took their buses home; meanwhile Emanuela waited, since the bus she should have taken was too crowded. That was the last time her friends saw her.

When Emanuela failed to return home, her father, Ercole Orlandi, a lay employee in the prefecture of the Papal State, together with her only brother Pietro, set off to look for her. They started at the music school and its vicinity. They also contacted some of her music school companions, but still failed to locate her. Thinking it might be a teenager's attempt to get attention, the school director advised Emanuela's father to wait and see if she turned up later in the evening before reporting her missing. Ignoring this, as he knew his daughter well, Ercole Orlandi went straight to the Trevi police station in Piazza del Collegio Romano to inform them about what had happened. The following morning, Natalina, another of Emanuela's sisters, filed a formal statement of her disappearance at the Vatican police station.

The family took its appeal to two Roman newspapers the next day. Emanuela's disappearance was announced to the public, with a recent photograph of her published; a phone number was also included for contacting the family. The next day, phone calls began pouring in with wild stories. When callers were asked to provide supporting evidence for their claims, they had none. As expected, the claims were spurious, often the work of mythomaniacs seeking publicity and a moment in the spotlight.

A few days after the disappearance, Emanuela's brother Pietro, along with some of his friends, discovered that two people had seen a young girl who looked very much like Emanuela talking to a man. They were considered reliable witnesses since one was a policeman and the other a traffic officer on duty outside the Senate. The latter, when questioned by the police, said the girl was with a thirty-five to forty-year-old male of medium height and thin build, with a long face and balding head. He was well-dressed, carried a case or some sort of rucksack, and had arrived in a green BMW. A friend of one of the Orlandis' cousins who belonged to the Italian secret service (SISDE) managed to trace the vehicle, or rather a mechanic who had recently replaced a small front side window that had been broken. A blonde woman had brought the car in for repair. Thanks to his contacts, the secret service agent soon found the woman, but she refused to cooperate. When he returned to his office, he learned that his investigations had already been reported to and discounted by his superiors. So this line of enquiry also dried up.

From the beginning of their tragedy up to this day, the Orlandi family has continued to seek support in its search from the Vatican, which has not always been forthcoming with it. However, on Sunday, July 3, 1983, during his Angelus address, the then-reigning Polish Pope, John Paul II, appealed for the first time to Emanuela's captors and called for her release, thus publicly revealing the probability that she had been kidnapped. His Holiness would repeat this appeal another seven times, all to no avail. Instead, this would be the beginning of what would become a seemingly never-ending stream of wild-goose chases, each more absurd than the last.

International Terrorism

At about eight in the evening on July 5, the Vatican's press office received an unexpected phone call. It came from a man who spoke Italian with a very strong American accent, which would be the reason why the press dubbed him the "*Americano.*" He confirmed that he and his organization were holding Emanuela and stated that he wanted to open negotiations with the Vatican through a dedicated phone line with the Secretary of the Vatican State, Cardinal Agostino Casaroli, who at that moment was on a visit to Poland. The man said he was calling regarding the case of Mehmet Ali Ağca, who was serving a life sentence for shooting and badly wounding Pope John Paul II in St. Peter's Square in Rome on May 13, 1981. His organization was demanding Ağca's release by July 20 in exchange for Emanuela. Its members, like Ağca, were part of the Grey Wolves, a violent Turkish right-wing organization known to be fundamentalist in its Islamic faith, ultra-nationalist, and neo-fascist.

Three days later, a man with a Middle Eastern accent, whose Italian pronunciation was poor, telephoned one of Emanuela's music school companions, telling her that her friend was their captive and the authorities had twenty days to free Mehmet Ali Ağca.

On July 17, following an anonymous call to the Italian news agency ANSA, a tape was found on the steps of the Quirinale presidential palace in Rome, confirming the demand for the Ağca exchange. But, more alarmingly, the voice of a young girl desperately calling for help could be heard on the recording. According to media reports, Emanuela's uncle, Mario Meneguzzi, said he believed it was his niece's voice on a portion of the tape, pleading to be allowed to sleep. Other anguished appeals appeared to have been spoken by another person with a higher-pitched voice that, in the end, proved to be dialogue taken from the audio portion of a film involving torture. This was probably aimed at terrorizing the family and enticing the public to pressure authorities to meet their demands.

The next day, the dedicated phone line was installed at the Vatican. Several days later, the *Americano* rang again, asking for Emanuela's uncle to make the message on the tape public, as well as to let the public know about the Grey Wolves's contact with Cardinal Casaroli. But the phone calls did not end there. The Roman newspaper *Il Messaggero* also received an anonymous call containing the first explicit threat that Emanuela would be killed on July 20 if the Pope's attacker was not freed. In all, the *Americano*, who has never been identified, made sixteen telephone calls, all from public phone boxes. A profile of him was made, though it wasn't released until 1995. Prepared by the second-in-command of the Italian secret service, it suggested that the identity of the man corresponded closely to that of Chicago-born archbishop Paul Marcinkus due to his knowledge of the workings of the Vatican, his knowledge of Latin, and his familiarity with certain areas of Rome. The good archbishop, then president of the IOR (Institute for the Works of Religion, commonly known as the Vatican Bank), would later become implicated in the scandal involving the bank in the wake of the death of another banker, Roberto Calvi of the Banco Ambrosiano, which had a close relationship with the Vatican—so much so that Calvi had been dubbed "God's banker." Calvi's mysterious death from hanging, which took place at London's Blackfriars Bridge in June 1982, has been the subject of countless conspiracy theories. The assumption about Marcinkus was never proven, nor was any evidence for the *Americano*'s claims that the Grey Wolves held Emanuela ever produced or found.

On November 20, 1984, in their twentieth communication, the Grey Wolves stated that they were holding both Emanuela and another fifteen-year-old girl, Mirella Gregori, who had disappeared in Rome a month before Emanuela.

Because Ağca's arrest had led to the November 25, 1982, arrest of his accomplice, a Bulgarian citizen named Sergei Antonov, it later emerged, during hearings on the attempted assassination of the Pope, that, as early as August 1982, Bulgaria may have been involved. It also emerged that Bulgarian authorities had sought the assistance of the Stasi, the security agency of the former East Germany, to deflect suspicion from the Bulgarian government's possible involvement in the Pope's shooting. Günther Bohnsack, a Stasi official, gave evidence that the East German secret services had used the Orlandi case to write false letters to Rome supporting the theory that Ağca was part of the Grey Wolves, thus distancing Bulgaria from any involvement. As one of the leading investigating judges commented, "What is profoundly painful is that, to this end (which can well be called the reasons of State), two young lives have been sacrificed."

In February 2010, Pietro Orlandi, who has dedicated his life to searching for his sister, secured two meetings, each less than an hour long, with Ağca at a secret location about fifty kilometers from Istanbul. Not a free man, the former terrorist affirmed that the kidnapping was organized by the Italian secret police in collaboration with the CIA, the US national security agency, on behalf of the Vatican, though he emphasized that the Pope knew nothing about the kidnapping. Ağca confirmed that Eastern European agencies had been involved in incidents aimed at distracting attention from any possible implication that any country or countries of the former Communist Bloc may have been culpable for the girl's disappearance. Above all, he stated that Emanuela was still alive, saying, "Emanuela is not suffering, she has never been badly treated. She is very well…." He believed she was somewhere in Europe, where "she now lives in isolation in a huge villa in France or Switzerland. She will return home."

A similar claim had been made in the year 2000 by Ferdinando Imposimato, a magistrate who has been involved in investigating a variety of Mafia and terrorist cases. He believed that Orlandi was living in a Muslim community, saying "Emanuela Orlandi is still alive and living in Turkey with her partner, who was one of her kidnappers. She was firstly taken to Germany, then to France, and finally to Turkey. She is now no longer interested in showing up; her life is elsewhere." So far there is little basis to these claims, as no one has actually seen her since that spring day in 1983, so they appear to be just more "red herrings" in an ever-growing list.

The Magliana Gang

One of the most spectacular claims regarding Emanuela's disappearance came in the form of an anonymous phone call on July 11, 2005, to the studio of the popular weekly national television program *Chi l'ha visto?* (*Who's Seen Him/Her?*). The caller claimed that, if they wanted to solve the Orlandi mystery, all they needed to do was to see who was buried in a diamond-encrusted tomb inside the Basilica of Sant'Apollinare in the center of Rome, located beside the Opus Dei University of the Holy Cross. The caller also said to look into "the favor that Renatino had done Cardinal Poletti." On further investigation, the body in the tomb turned out to be none other than forty-six-year-old Enrico De Pedis, known as "Renatino," the violent mobster and boss of the Magliana gang, who was shot down in a 1990 gangland killing close to the Campo de' Fiori in Rome. Founded in 1975, the gang was given its name by the media, since Magliana was the neighborhood in Rome many of its members came from. It specialized in drug dealing, illegal gambling, and large-scale money laundering. Its once-charismatic don De Pedis had, in fact, been permitted to be buried in this prestigious basilica on the authorization of Cardinal Ugo Poletti, then-president of the Italian Bishops Conference, apparently in return for an enormous donation the gangster's grieving widow had made to the church.

In 2007, Antonio Mancini, a former member of the Magliana gang turned police informer, confirmed in an interview with the same TV program that the girl was theirs, and "one of ours took her." This was later backed up by Maurizio Abbatino, another member of the gang and an informer; in 2009, he told magistrates that De Pedis and his men were involved in the kidnapping and killing of the girl, indicating that some unnamed members of the Vatican were also involved.

In 2008, Sabrina Minardi, who had been in a romantic relationship with De Pedis between spring 1982 and November 1984, told magistrates that the gang had kidnapped Emanuela, then killed her, putting her body in a bag and throwing it into a cement mixer, Mafia-style, in Torvaianica, a town on the outskirts of Rome. She said Renatino told her it had been done following the orders of Archbishop Marcinkus in order to send some kind of a message to "someone higher up." Her declarations brought strong protests from the Vatican, which accused her of a "lack of humanity and respect for the Orlandi family" and called her accusations "defaming...against Archbishop Marcinkus, who has been dead for some time and is unable to defend himself." While believing some of her story was plausible and supported by evidence, investigators were, in the end, not totally convinced.

A July 2011 interview with Antonio Mancini in *La Stampa* newspaper proved more convincing. He again stated that Emanuela Orlandi had been kidnapped by the gang for the purpose of obtaining restitution of Mafia money they had invested in the IOR through Banco Ambrosiano, adding that it was much more than twenty billion lire, which was never returned. Nonetheless, De Pedis had the attacks on the Vatican stopped in exchange for the right to be buried in the Basilica of Sant'Apollinare.

On May 14, 2012, Italian police opened De Pedis's tomb and took DNA samples. No sign of Emanuela or Mirella or anything related to them was found in the grave. Three years later, the cases of the two girls were closed and archived as unsolved.

Victim of Pedophiles

Of all the strange and bizarre characters that appear on the stage of the Orlandi drama, one of the most colorful is that of Italian priest and chief exorcist of the Roman Catholic Diocese of Rome, Father Gabriele Amorth, who is reported to have performed an estimated 160,000 exorcisms during his sixty-plus years as a priest. In an interview he gave to *La Stampa* in May 2012, the eighty-seven-year-old prelate proclaimed that Emanuela had been lured to one of the sexual orgies of pedophile exponents of the clergy and members of the foreign diplomatic corps to the Vatican. He maintained that she was probably drugged and then killed, and her body concealed to avoid their exposure. He also repeated his claims in his book *L'ultimo Esorcista* (*The Last Exorcist*).

An earlier claim like this had also been made by an anonymous source in 2005, except with the variant that the girl may have been "accidentally" killed during one of these sex and drug-fueled parties. This time, the tragedy supposedly took place at the residence of a high-ranking priest or individual close to the Vatican in his palazzo near the Gianicolo, not far from the terminus of the bus Emanuela would have taken to return home. The source said she was buried within the Vatican grounds in the same place as other hapless young victims of these same gatherings. No eyewitness or corroborated evidence has ever turned up to prove that any of these theories is true. Perhaps it may well be interpreted by some to be, in the words of Father Amorth, "the work of the devil."

The Question Remains: "Why?"

Even after all these years, why does this unsolved mystery of Emanuela's presumed kidnapping remain so seared into the Italian consciousness, with rumors proposing new theories and possible scenarios of what really happened to her appearing from time to time? If Mirella Gregori, the other teen who disappeared a month before Emanuela, is remembered at all in the press or elsewhere, it's because she is almost always seen as an appendage to the Orlandi case, rather than as an individual in her own right who met a tragic end of some kind. So what is at the basis of this fascination with Emanuela's fate? In my view, the only answer is its connection to the Vatican. For centuries, the walls surrounding this state within a state have kept its secrets. They have guarded them well with the help of the Vatican's colorful Swiss guards and its own separate police force and diplomatic corps.

And yet the Vatican still has had its scandals and mysteries within mysteries. Two recent examples will suffice. The first relates to the sudden and seemingly inexplicable death of the "smiling" Pope, John Paul I. After the death of Pope Paul VI, Cardinal Albino Luciani had been elevated to the position of pope on August 26, 1978. He was the first pope in the history of the papacy to take two names but, despite the length of his new name, his was to be the shortest pontificate since the death of the Medici pope, Leo XI, in April 1605. Just thirty-three days after his election, Luciani was found dead in bed. It was announced officially that he had died of a heart attack, but the suddenness of his demise and the discrepancies in reports about the exact time of death fanned suspicion. In 1984, British journalist and writer David Yollop published a book entitled *In God's Name: An Investigation into the Murder of Pope John Paul I*. In it, he argued that Luciani had been murdered because of fears that he would expose existing ties between the Vatican, the Mafia, and the deviant Freemason lodge P2 (*Propaganda Due*), as well as reveal the corrupt links between Archbishop Paul Marcinkus, the Vatican Bank, and the Archdiocese of Chicago. Under the leadership of financier Licio Gelli, the P2 turned into a clandestine radical-right organization that contravened Article 18 of the Italian Constitution on banned secret associations. It was implicated in numerous Italian cases, including the collapse of the Vatican-affiliated Banco Ambrosiano, the murder of journalist Carmine "Mino" Pecorelli, and the death of banker Roberto Calvi, as well as corruption cases within the nationwide bribe scandal known as Tangentopoli. The lodge's activities were discovered when the collapse of banker Michele Sindona's financial empire was investigated. To put an end to this mounting speculation, the Vatican commissioned its own investigation in 1987. Headed by British academic and investigative journalist John Cornwell, the inquiry's conclusion was that there was no conspiracy, and Luciani had died of a pulmonary embolism caused by overwork and stress.

Other strange circumstances arose following the appointment of Alois Estermann as commander of the Pontifical Swiss Guard on May 4, 1998. Only a matter of hours later on that very same day, Estermann and his wife, Gladys Meza Romero, were found dead in their Vatican City flat. They had allegedly been shot to death by twenty-three-year-old Swiss Guard Cédric Tornay, who then turned the gun on himself. The official Vatican version given for the motive was that the culprit was disgruntled due to having been denied a military decoration. A 2002 book entitled *Assassinati in Vaticano* (*Murdered in the Vatican*) by French lawyers Luc Brossollet and Jacques Vergès disputes this; they maintain that Tornay was killed and the scene concocted to look like a murder-suicide. Theories abound, though the official version remains.

Therefore, it is no wonder that what goes on behind those venerable, ancient walls constantly titillates the imagination and whets the public's curiosity. My guess is that it will continue to do so until Emanuela is finally found, either alive or dead.

In a Field Outside of Edmonton

Janel Comeau

It was the afternoon of August 3, 1997, and Kathy King couldn't find her daughter.

Kathy, a registered social worker, had a regular weekly routine with her twenty-two-year-old daughter Caralyn, who preferred to go by "Cara." Once a week, the pair would meet up at their usual spot, and Kathy would take her daughter out for a meal before buying her groceries and taking her clothes shopping. Cara had gotten off to a rough start in adulthood, and this was Kathy's way of making sure her daughter always had the things she needed.

But on this particular day, Cara never turned up.

At first, Kathy didn't worry. Like many young people her age, Cara struggled with time management. This was the late 1990s, before there was a cellphone in every hand and an internet connection in every home—it simply wasn't unusual to be out of contact with loved ones for hours, days, or even weeks on end. Kathy simply assumed their meeting had slipped her daughter's mind.

But when Cara missed a scheduled court appearance two days later, Kathy began to worry. And when a friend of Cara's reached out, saying she hadn't seen or heard from Cara in several days, Kathy knew something was terribly wrong. She spent the next few days tracking down

Cara's friends and acquaintances to see if anyone knew where she was, but no one had heard from her since August 2.

On August 9, Kathy King walked into a police station to report her daughter missing.

To her surprise, police refused to take her report. Cara was a known sex worker who struggled with a cocaine addiction. At the time of her disappearance, she had been staying at a local women's shelter. The outgoing, happy-go-lucky attitude that made Cara the light of her mother's life had also led her to take some dangerous risks as a teenager, and she quickly fell in with the wrong crowd. She'd left home at eighteen and had begun working in the sex trade shortly afterward to feed her burgeoning addiction. By age twenty-two, she was bouncing between friends' couches and beds in local women's shelters, punctuated with occasional stays in psychiatric facilities to address mental health issues and drug-induced psychotic episodes. Her mother was sometimes able to secure apartments for her, but Cara's ongoing struggles meant she was quickly evicted and back out on the streets.

To Kathy King, Cara was a beloved daughter experiencing some personal struggles, and her disappearance was an immediate cause for alarm. The police, who were familiar with Cara after arresting her twice for solicitation, did not treat her disappearance with nearly the same urgency. Kathy was told to check hospitals and jail cells and was turned away without a report being filed.

Two days later, Kathy was back. She had done as they asked but had found no trace of Cara. Once again, however, police turned her away without taking a report. Although it had now been nine days since anyone had seen or spoken with Cara, police still believed there was no cause for concern. Without concrete evidence of foul play, they felt there was no need for the police to be involved.

Desperate, Kathy King began to investigate her daughter's disappearance on her own. She took to the downtown streets her daughter was known to frequent, passing out homemade missing-person flyers and putting up posters with her daughter's picture. No one came forward with information about Cara's whereabouts.

Kathy returned to the police station. On August 23, she was finally given a file number for her daughter's official missing persons case. She asked the officer who took the report about the next steps police would take in trying to locate her daughter.

"Now we wait for a body to turn up."

Kathy asked if he was joking.

He wasn't.

And as it turned out, they didn't have to wait long.

On September 2, 1997, Kathy King opened her newspaper and saw a photo of first responders carrying a white body bag out of a farmer's field outside the city. The body was badly decomposed, and police were not immediately able to identify who it belonged to. Kathy believed she knew. She called police and asked if Cara's dental records could be compared to the remains that had been found.

She got a call the following day. The body in the field was Cara's.

But just as quickly as the formal investigation into Cara's death was opened, it was over. Cara's cause of death was inconclusive; much of the damage to her bones was determined to be posthumous and caused by scavenging animals. The length of time her body had lain outdoors in the elements had destroyed the evidence that might have revealed the circumstances of her death. Kathy King was provided with a copy of her daughter's autopsy on the condition she not reveal any information that could compromise the ongoing investigation. Kathy has held true to her word and kept the contents of the autopsy a secret but admits there really isn't much to tell. No suspects were named, and no one was ever charged with the murder of Caralyn King. The case went cold before it had even begun to heat up.

Despite her family's best efforts, Cara's case seemed destined to fade into obscurity. Hers was not the sort of case to ignite the interest of late-night true crime television shows—she was a young woman who lived and worked on the streets and had fallen victim to violence. The media might have forgotten her entirely, except for one thing—another body turned up in similar circumstances in a rural area outside of town.

Then another.

And another.

And another.

———————

Cara King lived and vanished in the city of Edmonton, located at the heart of the Canadian province of Alberta. Home to nearly one million people, the city is perhaps best known for being the site of the West Edmonton Mall, once the largest shopping mall on the planet. It's also the home of the Edmonton Oilers hockey team, the NHL team that Wayne Gretzky led to four Stanley Cup championships over the course of his storied career.

But the city of Edmonton also holds a far more dubious honor—it consistently has one of the highest homicide rates of any major city in the country, sometimes claiming the title "Murder Capital of Canada." There is no one reason why Edmonton has such a problem with homicide—signs leading into the city read "City of Champions" not "Commit Murder Here"—but there is a complex web of factors that set the stage for women to start disappearing from the streets in droves.

For starters, there's the matter of Edmonton's geographical isolation. Outside the city limits lies nothing but sparsely populated farms and wilderness for hundreds of kilometers in all directions. Edmontonians have a tendency to measure distance in the number of hours it takes to drive somewhere—this is the simplest way to communicate distance in a place where you can drive for two hours in any direction and still end up in the middle of nowhere. Calgary, the closest major city to the south, is three hours away. To the north lies Fort McMurray, just over four hours away. To the east is Saskatoon, located in the province of Saskatchewan, five hours away. And to the west, there's practically nothing—hours upon hours of Alberta wilderness that simply gives on to hours upon hours of British Columbia wilderness, nearly all the way to the coast. A person looking to dump a body in a remote area outside of Edmonton would find themselves positively spoiled for options.

Edmonton is also bisected by the Yellowhead Highway, a segment of the Trans-Canada Highway that runs from Winnipeg, Manitoba, to Masset, British Columbia. Officially, this road is known as Highway 16. A segment of the British Columbia section of the road, however, bears a different name—it is widely known as "the Highway of Tears." It gained this somber nickname after more than eighty women—mostly young and Indigenous—went missing or were murdered along its length between the early 1970s and the early 2020s. Though no firm connection has ever been made between the missing women of the Highway of Tears and the missing women of downtown Edmonton, drivers traveling along the highway would pass through the north end of Edmonton—the same area where most of Edmonton's missing women were last seen.

Lastly—and perhaps most importantly—Edmonton is home to one of the largest urban Indigenous populations anywhere in Canada. More than 6 percent of the city's population identify as Indigenous; by comparison, Toronto's Indigenous community make up just 0.7 percent of the city's population. Indigenous people living in Canadian urban centers often find themselves disenfranchised, struggling with both the generational traumas of Canada's abusive residential school programs and the ongoing racism faced by Indigenous Canadians. This population regularly experiences discrimination in housing, employment, education, and the justice system, leaving the community under-resourced, over-policed, and disproportionately likely to end up becoming the victims of violence.

Indigenous women account for roughly 4 percent of the Canadian female population, but, as of 2015, they made up 24 percent of female homicide victims.

But whatever lay at the heart of Edmonton's epidemic of missing women—whether it was economics, geography, lifestyle, race, or some complex combination of the above—there was no denying that, at the dawn of the twenty-first century, women started going missing from Edmonton at alarming rates.

Six weeks after the discovery of Cara King's body, the body of twenty-two-year-old Joyce Ann Hewitt was found in a field in Sherwood Park. Like Cara, Joyce had lived a high-risk lifestyle on the streets of Edmonton prior to her disappearance and had been suspected of being involved in the sex trade.

In the year 2000, the family of Linda May Scott began to get worried. Linda, a twenty-nine-year-old mother of five, had been living a high-risk lifestyle on the streets of Edmonton and Vancouver for some time, but had made contact with her family at least once per month. Now, however, they had stopped hearing from her entirely. Adopted from the Blood Indian Reserve as an infant, Linda had been in the process of learning more about her Indigenous roots and filing paperwork to reconnect with her biological family when she suddenly disappeared. No trace of her has ever been found.

On January 27, 2001, a resident out for a walk near Villeneuve discovered a body lying near an open gravel pit. The body belonged to Kelly Dawn Reilly, a twenty-four-year-old mother who had gone missing just under two weeks earlier on January 15. Kelly was suspected to work in the sex trade. Her case garnered little media attention.

In the early hours of September 9, 2002, a young woman named Deanna Bellerose was standing on the corner of 95 Street and 105 A Avenue with a friend. Twenty-nine-year-old Deanna was an Indigenous mother of four children, whom she cared for very much. In fall 2002, she was supporting herself through sex work. Family members said she'd begun making plans to exit street life and was looking at checking herself into a treatment center so she could begin the process of attempting to regain custody of her children. Sadly, she never got the chance. She got into a car that morning and was not seen alive again. It would take ten years for her family to learn her ultimate fate—her skeletal remains were discovered by a land surveyor in a rural area near Morinville on May 16, 2012.

On September 22, 2002, twenty-eight-year-old Edna Bernard—an Indigenous mother who doted on her six boys—went out for a night on the town. She was last seen by a friend, who watched her get into a car with several strangers outside a nightclub in the wee hours of the morning. Her burnt body was discovered in a farmer's field in Leduc the following day. It was determined that all her fingers had been broken, and she had been strangled before being set on fire. Over the next thirteen years, the bodies of three more women would be found in roughly the same area.

On November 4, 2002, another twenty-nine-year-old Indigenous mother named Debbie Darlene Lake stepped out of her home in the early hours of the morning. Debbie had fallen in with the wrong crowd in high school and had left school at eighteen without completing her diploma. Now twenty-nine, Debbie was a married cancer survivor and the mother of a ten-month-old baby; she and her husband were living out of a bus with their infant as they worked on stabilizing their lives. When she left their home on November 4, she was heading down the street to call a friend from a payphone—she planned to be back so quickly she did not even bring her cigarettes. Debbie, however, never returned. Her husband reported her missing the following day. Her remains would be found in a remote area near Miquelon Lake on April 12, 2003, by a man who'd been out looking for deer antlers.

Monique Pitre, a thirty-year-old Indigenous woman, worked in the sex trade and was struggling with an addiction to cocaine. On the evening of November 5, 2002, her roommate dropped her off at the Transit Hotel, an establishment of somewhat ill repute in the northeast end of the city. It was the last time her roommate would see her alive—

Monique's remains were discovered weeks later on January 8, 2003, in an unincorporated rural area outside the city.

Sometime in 2002, the family of thirty-four-year-old Lynn Minia Jackson stopped hearing from her. Since she was estranged from her family, they were not concerned about the lack of contact. In 2002, she was known to be working in the Edmonton sex trade to survive. On June 21, 2004, a group of hikers discovered her remains off a hiking trail in Wetaskiwin.

In most circumstances, this many back-to-back disappearances would have an entire city on high alert. Parents all over the world kept a closer eye on their children for decades after six-year-old Adam Walsh was abducted from a Sears department store in South Florida and murdered in 1981, citing his case as the reason for their caution; his case led to the founding of the National Center for Missing & Exploited Children and drove his father, John Walsh, to create the television show *America's Most Wanted*. But the murders and disappearances of more than a dozen women failed to make much of an impression on the city of Edmonton. In many cases, these crimes barely made it into the back pages of the newspaper.

There is a well-known phenomenon in criminology called "Missing White Woman Syndrome," which is more or less exactly what it sounds like. In the media, there's a tendency to grant disproportionate coverage to cases of missing White women and girls while largely ignoring cases that involve men or women of color. More than a decade after her disappearance, there are people all over the world who could draw the face of missing British toddler Madeleine McCann from memory. Mention the names Asha Degree or Rahma el-Dennaoui—two non-White young girls who disappeared from the United States and Australia respectively, in similar circumstances at around the same time—and the only thing most people can draw is a blank.

Race and gender, of course, aren't the only factors at play when it comes to media coverage; lifestyle and socioeconomic status have a role as well. The more "unlikely" the victim, the more coverage her disappearance receives. A missing suburban housewife with a perfect marriage and perfect family can dominate the airwaves for weeks on end, while a missing sex worker with substance abuse issues will struggle to make the local news even in her own town.

Canada is not immune to "Missing White Woman Syndrome." A 2008 study published in *The Law and Society Association* journal found that within Canada, missing White women receive twenty-seven times more national media coverage than missing Indigenous women. The same study also found marked differences in the quality of media coverage. Stories about missing Indigenous women tended to be dispassionate and lacking in detail, while stories about missing White women used more emotional language, emphasized the innocence of the victim, and spent more time exploring the impact of the woman's disappearance on her loved ones and community. In other words, a missing White woman is treated as a tragedy. A missing Indigenous woman is simply a statistic.

News coverage of Edmonton's missing and murdered women was less than flattering. Stories tended to highlight their addictions, their legal troubles, and their work in their sex trade—it was not uncommon for newspapers to refer to them as "hookers." Many of the missing women were mothers, and the media rarely missed an opportunity to make disparaging comments about their perceived failures as parents. One article noted that Kelly Dawn Reilly had failed to "return from a night of prostitution and drugs in time to care for her five-year-old girl," presenting Kelly's violent murder at the age of twenty-four as though it were predominantly an attempt to wriggle out of her parenting responsibilities.

It seemed as though there was no death toll that would make authorities and local media take the disappearances of these women seriously. But then, in the first decade of the twenty-first century, the issue of missing and murdered Indigenous women came roaring into the headlines in a way no one could ignore.

The year was 2002, and the most prolific serial killer in Canadian history was about to be brought down by an asthma inhaler.

In the course of a little over two decades, beginning in the late 1970s, more than sixty-five women disappeared from the Downtown Eastside neighborhood of Vancouver, British Columbia. These missing women had a great deal in common with their Edmonton counterparts—they too, were known or suspected sex workers. Most struggled with addiction. Many were veterans of the British Columbia foster care system, a system they'd abruptly "aged out" of on their nineteenth birthdays. The vast majority were Indigenous, hailing from First Nations or Métis (mixed European and Indigenous ancestry) communities. They were, in law enforcement terms, "high-risk" individuals—their lifestyles put them at an elevated risk of falling victim to violence or early death.

And, overwhelmingly, the police did not seem to care that they were missing.

Concerned friends, family members, and social services workers who attempted to file missing persons reports with the Vancouver Police Department often found themselves facing the same obstacles Kathy King had faced—police simply weren't interested in the disappearance of so-called "high-risk" women. Oftentimes, police would simply refuse to take a report at all. Worried parents, siblings, and partners were told their missing loved one was likely off on a bender and would turn up eventually, even when family insisted it was out of character for her to be out of contact this long. Days, weeks, months, and even years would tick by with no contact—and still the Vancouver police insisted that these cases were simply not worth investigating.

In one instance, the family of Elsie Sebastian, a forty-year-old Indigenous mother of four, last saw their loved one in October 1992. When they attempted to file a missing persons report in 1993, however, Vancouver police refused to formally open a case. Two more attempts were made in 1994 and 1999, but police declined to take a formal missing persons report each time. It wasn't until 2001—nine years after Elsie Sebastian was last seen or heard from—when police finally agreed to open a missing persons case. Her family are still waiting to learn her fate.

For years, there had been whispers circulating through the Downtown Eastside about Robert "Willie" Pickton, a local pig farmer who owned a large farm near Port Coquitlam, just outside the city. Women who went out to Pickton's farm had a tendency to disappear. Pickton had actually been arrested for the attempted murder of a young sex worker in 1997. Prosecutors ultimately opted to drop the charges against him, saying that his victim's drug addiction made her an unreliable witness—this was despite the fact that she was found on the night of the attempted murder with handcuffs locked to her wrists, the key to which was located in Pickton's pocket.

When police finally arrived on the Pickton farm in February 2002, they were not there for missing women—they were there to execute a search warrant for illegal firearms. One of the officers conducting the search happened to open a sports bag containing an asthma inhaler; it was prescribed to Sereena Abotsway, a woman who had disappeared in August 2001. Police soon found other personal effects belonging to missing women. There were numerous shoes, clothes, purses, and jewelry, many of which could be directly tied to women who'd vanished from the Downtown Eastside. Most importantly, the police also discovered victims' DNA on the farm. In total, twenty-six missing women could be conclusively linked to evidence found on the pig farm. Pickton confessed to murdering a total of forty-nine women, lamenting that he had not been able to make it an even fifty.

Perhaps most horrifically, victims' DNA was found on an industrial meat grinder located on the farm. Authorities believe Pickton may have disposed of some of his victims by putting them through the meat grinder, eventually mixing their remains into sausage that was sold in the Vancouver area.

The discovery of human remains on Willie Pickton's pig farm was a moment of vindication for the families of the victims—and it was a moment of acute shame for the Vancouver Police Department and for Canadian law enforcement as a whole. The case exploded in the news, and people around the world expressed their outrage toward the Vancouver PD. If Vancouver police had taken reports of missing Indigenous women and sex workers more seriously, people wondered, how quickly could they have spotted the pattern among these disappearances? And, most importantly, how many women might they have saved from meeting a violent end?

Robert Pickton was convicted on six counts of second-degree murder in December 2007. His incarceration did little to redeem the image of policing in Canada. Vancouver police had allowed one of the most prolific serial killers in modern history to operate freely for more than two decades. Police themselves had purchased ground pork believed to be contaminated with human flesh.

Determined not to repeat the same mistakes they'd made in Vancouver, the RCMP turned their sights to Alberta, another hotbed of missing women.

The hunt for a serial killer was on.

It was May 2006, and a man named Thomas Svekla had just shown up for a visit at his sister's house with a heavy hockey bag in tow.

Svekla, a thirty-eight-year-old mechanic, cautioned his family not to open the hockey bag. He claimed it was filled with compost worms;

this was his explanation for why the bag appeared very heavy. Svekla's sister noticed her brother was very protective of the hockey bag—too protective, she thought, for a bag supposedly filled with worms. The moment he left the bag unattended, she and her husband hurried to open it.

Inside she found not compost worms, but the body of a thirty-six-year-old woman named Theresa Innes.

Theresa Innes, who had vanished from the streets of downtown Edmonton nearly two months earlier, had been tightly wrapped in a deflated air mattress and a shower curtain, and bound with long coils of wire. She was so tightly wrapped Svekla's sister initially didn't understand what she was looking at. She would later testify in court that it took her a moment to understand that the curved plastic object in front of her was actually a plastic-wrapped human body. Svekla's sister and her husband immediately called the police. When coroners arrived on the scene, it took them more than an hour to free Theresa Innes's body from the elaborate cocoon of wire and plastic she'd been entrapped in.

Thomas Svekla was quickly arrested for murder.

From the outside, there seemed to be nothing sinister about Thomas Svekla. In photographs, he appears to be of average height and build, with thinning dark hair and a plain, unremarkable face. Born to hardworking farmers in the town of Vegreville, Alberta, in 1968, Svekla was the youngest of seven children, growing up with six older sisters. As a child he was reportedly polite, helpful, and well-mannered, often helping out on neighbors' farms. By his early forties, he was leading a perfectly ordinary life as a professional mechanic and a divorced father of one. But as his murder trial unfolded, it was revealed that there was much more to Svekla—from an early age, he seemed to have the makings of a serial killer.

Svekla's parents, George and Emily, were a salt-of-the-earth couple who'd been married for fifty years at the time of their only son's arrest. Behind closed doors, however, theirs had been a troubled marriage.

George Svekla was said to struggle with alcoholism and often became violent; in a divorce petition filed by Emily Svekla in spring 1980, she'd accused him of kicking her in the back with steel-toed boots so hard she needed surgery. She also said he savagely beat the children, choking them, hitting them in the face, whipping them with belt buckles, and kicking them so ferociously they were left bloodied and in need of surgical intervention. Emily, however, did not go through with the divorce. As Thomas Svekla himself later testified, his mother was unable to leave the marriage due to her financial circumstances. When George agreed to check himself into a rehabilitation program, she dropped the petition for divorce and reconciled with him.

To make up for staying with her abusive husband, Emily coddled her only son. In his own words, his mother treated him like he could "do no wrong," even when he misbehaved. His sisters felt their mother was overprotective of Thomas. She attempted to shield him from the world, begging him not to leave the house and to stay with her instead.

But Thomas did go out into the world. And as it turned out, it wasn't Thomas who needed protection from the world—it was the world that needed protection from Thomas.

Thomas Svekla was fourteen years old when he committed his first recorded act of sexual violence. He pinned a school classmate to a wall, attempting to strip off her clothes as he did so. He would do the same thing at age seventeen. This time, he chased a friend's sister through her family home, eventually catching her and pinning her to the floor in an attempt to rape her. Shortly after graduating from high school, he choked his first serious girlfriend in a parking garage. He spent the remainder of his twenties engaged in crimes ranging from drunk driving and car theft to his 1993 conviction for assaulting a sex worker in Edmonton's downtown core.

At the age of twenty-seven, Svekla began a romantic relationship with a woman who was raising several foster children alongside her then nine-year-old biological daughter. Svekla began to sexually abuse one of the foster children, a five-year-old girl; he would trap the girl under a blanket while she was watching television with the other children and attack her while they looked on. When the abuse eventually came to light, he was jailed for his crimes. In a stunning twist of cruelty, Svekla phoned his ex-girlfriend from lockup to tell her that he had also sexually abused her biological daughter and taunted her by saying the five-year-old child had been more pleasing to him in bed.

After being released from prison for his crimes against the children, Svekla resumed his old patterns into his thirties—he drank, committed petty crimes, and partied with sex workers throughout Alberta. At some point, he met and befriended Theresa Innes, a mother of two from the remote northern town of High Level. Theresa supported herself by working in the town's thriving sex trade. High Level is home to a booming oil and gas industry, and men who move there for work often find themselves flush with cash but short on single young women. How Theresa Innes ended up deceased in Thomas Svekla's hockey bag in Fort Saskatchewan, nearly seven hundred kilometers away, is a mystery only Thomas Svekla can unravel. To date, he has provided very little information on the circumstances of her murder. Ultimately, courts did not need to hear Svekla's side of the story to be convinced of his guilt. He was convicted of the second-degree murder of Theresa Innes in 2008 and sentenced to seventeen years in prison.

Two years later, he was brought back before the courts and officially declared a "Dangerous Offender," a legal designation Canadian courts reserve for violent offenders who are deemed to have no hope of successful rehabilitation. As a Dangerous Offender, Svekla is subject to an indefinite prison sentence. He is currently incarcerated at the Edmonton Institution, one of Canada's few maximum-security correctional facilities. In all likelihood, he will die without ever taking another step outside its walls.

But in the course of investigating Svekla for the murder of Theresa Innes, authorities noticed something suspicious—Svekla had a connection to another murdered sex worker. In 2004, he had been the one to call in the mutilated body of nineteen-year-old Rachel Quinney, which he claimed to have discovered by accident in a field in a rural area of Sherwood Park. Svekla told authorities at the time that he had taken a local sex worker out for a walk in a field in the early hours of the morning to look for a private place to use drugs, and said they had accidentally stumbled upon the young woman's body. Svekla later told a prison cellmate that he had actually taken the sex worker into the remote field to murder her, but had been forced to abandon his plan when he'd accidentally taken her too close to Rachel's body, tripping over his previous victim in the dark. Svekla stood trial for the murder of Rachel Quinney. This time, however, the court did not feel there was enough evidence for a conviction, and Svekla was acquitted.

Svekla's connection to the Rachel Quinney case still piqued the interest of authorities. Dating back to the late 1980s, there had been a string of unsolved homicides in the Edmonton area that followed a similar pattern. The victims were sex workers, most of whom were Indigenous, and they tended to disappear from downtown Edmonton or along 118 Avenue, one of the city's most notorious prostitution strolls. Their bodies would invariably be found in a field outside of Edmonton, sometimes months or years after they disappeared. Authorities had long suspected that many of these homicides were the work of one person. At long last, they thought they'd found him.

In addition to the murder of Rachel Quinney, Svekla was considered an official suspect in at least five other homicides, including those of twenty-two-year-old Bernadette Ahenakew, twenty-eight-year-old Edna Bernard, twenty-nine-year-old Debbie Darlene Lake, and thirty-year-old Monique Pitre. He was also suspected in the disappearances of twenty-seven-year-old Corrie Renee Ottenbreit and thirty-two-year-old Delores Dawn Brower, both of whom disappeared within days of each other in spring 2004. Their bodies would not be discovered until 2015, when their skeletal remains were found dumped together in the same spot in rural Leduc.

Svekla would ultimately never stand trial for any of these murders. But at least, investigators thought, the man who'd terrorized the women of Edmonton was finally off the streets.

In late August 2008, months after Thomas Svekla had been remanded to prison custody, forty-four-year-old Annette Margaret Holywhiteman disappeared from the streets of Edmonton.

Annette's disappearance was reported by a social services agency in 2009. Her remains were discovered by horseback riders in 2010, dumped in a rural field near Westlock, just outside Edmonton. Like the other women, Annette was Indigenous and worked in the sex trade. Police had been reluctant to take a missing persons report due to her "high-risk" lifestyle.

A murderer was still on the loose in Edmonton.

Then in August 2010, a plane touched down at the Edmonton International Airport from Fort McMurray. Twenty-year-old Amber Tuccaro was aboard. The young Indigenous mother had flown to Edmonton with her infant son and a female friend, intending to have a fun vacation in the big city. The women had planned to spend their first night at a motel in Nisku, near the airport, then head into the city the following day. Amber, however, changed her mind. She accepted a ride into the city with an unknown man, promising her friend she would return later that night.

Amber never came back.

Friends and family attempted to report Amber's disappearance to the RCMP the following morning. Police, however, insisted she was likely out partying and they refused to take a report. Although they did eventually add her to the missing persons list, they quietly removed her a month later. The RCMP even went so far as to make an announcement on September 4, 2010, stating that they did not believe Amber Tuccaro to be in any danger.

Amber Tuccaro's remains were found in rural Leduc County on September 1, 2012.

In Amber's case, police had something they'd never had in any of the other homicide investigations—namely, the voice of her probable killer on tape. Amber had phoned her incarcerated brother while in the car with the unknown man, and the prison phone system had recorded the conversation. Police released sixty-one seconds of the recording to the public, hoping someone could identify the voice of the man who'd offered Amber a ride. In the recording, she can be heard asking him where he's taking her; in a suspicious tone, she tells him he had better not be taking her anywhere she doesn't want to go. The man, speaking with the same rural-lilted accent so many in the area share, reassures her that he is driving her into the city.

Though police released only sixty-one seconds of the recording, the full phone call was seventeen minutes long—almost exactly the amount of time it takes to drive from the motel where Amber was picked up to the site where her body was found. As Amber had suspected, she was being driven in the opposite direction from that which the man had claimed.

The clip of Amber's final phone call went viral in Canada and across the true crime community, leading to hope that the killer might be recognized and the mystery of Edmonton's killing fields might finally be solved after more than thirty years. The recording, however, did not turn up any viable leads.

The identity of the man who killed Amber—and Corrie, Edna, Cara, Monique, Bernadette, Delores, Brianna, Lynn, Annette, Kelly, Jessica, and so many others—remains unknown.

———————

As of September 2021, the following missing persons and murder cases in the city of Edmonton remain unsolved.

Unsolved Missing Persons Cases

Monica Cardinal, age forty-six
- Last seen leaving the International Hotel in Edmonton in June 1993

Michelle Jeanette Harmer, age twenty-nine
- Last seen at her home in Edmonton on November 15, 1995

Karen Jean Kozicki, age thirty-two
- Last seen leaving work in May 1996

Judy Desjarlais, age twenty-nine
- Last seen near the North Saskatchewan River on October 7, 1997

Lara Danielle Brown, age twenty-six
- Last had contact with friends on August 29, 1998

Linda May Scott, age twenty-nine
- Last had contact with family in 2000

Maggie Lee Burke, age twenty-one
- Last seen near 118 Avenue in Edmonton on December 9, 2004

Freda Whiteman, age fifty
- Last seen at the York Hotel in Edmonton on October 6, 2006

Michelle Louise Mercer, age forty-six
- Last seen in Edmonton on February 6, 2009

Roxanne Marie Isadore, age twenty-four
- Last seen in Edmonton in September 2007; possibly seen in Fort St. John, British Columbia, in February 2011

Marie Antoinette Carlson-Hill, age thirty-one
- Last seen in Edmonton on February 15, 2012

Shelly Dene, age twenty-five
- Last had contact with family in August 2013

Nicole "Nikki" Frenchman, age twenty-three
- Last seen getting into a truck in Edmonton on July 10, 2021

Unsolved Murders

Gail Cardinal, age twenty-one
- Remains discovered in a rural area ten kilometers south of Fort Saskatchewan in 1983

Georgette Flint, age twenty
- Last seen in Edmonton
- Remains discovered in a rural area west of Elk Island National Park on September 13, 1988

Bernadette Ahenakew, age twenty-two
- Last seen in Edmonton in September 1989
- Remains discovered in a ditch off a rural road near Sherwood Park on October 24, 1989

Mavis Mason, age twenty-nine
- Remains discovered near a rural road outside Edmonton on October 25, 1990

Jessica Cardinal, age twenty-four
- Last contacted her family from an Edmonton hospital on June 11, 1997
- Remains discovered behind a commercial building in Edmonton on June 13, 1997

Caralyn Aubrey King, age twenty-two
- Last seen in Edmonton on August 2, 1997
- Remains discovered in a field in Sherwood Park on September 1, 1997

Joyce Anne Hewitt, age twenty-two
- Remains discovered in a field in Sherwood Park on October 19, 1997

Kelly Dawn Reilly, age twenty-four
- Last seen in Edmonton on January 15, 2001
- Remains discovered behind a gravel pit near Villeneuve on January 27, 2001

Deanna Bellerose, age twenty-nine
- Last seen getting into a car on the corner of 95 Street and 105 A Avenue in downtown Edmonton on September 9, 2002
- Remains discovered in a field near Morinville on May 16, 2012

Edna Bernard, age twenty-eight
- Last seen getting into a car outside a nightclub on September 22, 2002
- Remains discovered in a farmer's field near Leduc on September 23, 2002

Monique Pitre, age thirty
- Last seen being dropped off in front of the Transit Hotel in northeast Edmonton on November 5, 2002
- Remains discovered in a field outside the city near Township Road 540 and Range Road 222 on January 8, 2003

Lynn Minia Jackson, thirty-four
- Last seen in Edmonton in 2002
- Remains discovered near a hiking trail in Wetaskiwin on June 21, 2004

Katie Ballantyne, age forty
- Last seen in Edmonton on April 27, 2003
- Remains discovered in a farmer's field near Leduc on July 7, 2003

Corrie Renee Ottenbreit, age twenty-seven
- Last seen leaving the home she shared with her husband and child in Edmonton on May 9, 2004
- Remains discovered on a rural property near Leduc on April 19, 2015

Delores Dawn Brower, age thirty-two

- Last seen hitchhiking in downtown Edmonton in the early hours of May 13, 2004
- Remains discovered on a rural property near Leduc on April 19, 2015

Rachel Quinney, age nineteen

- Last seen in Edmonton on May 28, 2004
- Remains found in a wooded area near Sherwood Park on June 11, 2004

Rene Lynn Gunning, age nineteen

- Last seen at the West Edmonton Mall on February 18, 2005
- Remains discovered by campers in a rural area near Grande Prairie on May 21, 2011

Krystle Ann Julia Knott, age sixteen

- Last seen at the West Edmonton Mall on February 18, 2005
- Remains discovered by campers in a rural area near Grande Prairie on May 21, 2011

Bonnie Lynn Jack, age thirty-seven

- Last seen in Edmonton in February 2006
- Remains discovered in a rural area east of Edmonton in May 2006

Leanne Lori Benwell, age twenty-seven

- Last seen in downtown Edmonton on March 24, 2007
- Remains discovered in a rural field near Wetaskiwin on June 21, 2007

Brianna Danielle Torvalson, age twenty-one
  • Remains found in the driveway of an acreage near Township
    Road 534 and Range Road 220 in rural Strathcona County
    on February 21, 2008

Annette Margaret Holywhiteman, age forty-four
  • Last seen in Edmonton in late summer 2008
  • Remains discovered on a rural property near Westlock in
    November 2010

Leslie Ann Talley, age twenty-nine
  • Remains found in the snow beside a truck near the corner of
    151 Avenue and 31 Street in Edmonton on January 6, 2010

Amber Tuccaro, age twenty
  • Last seen hitchhiking in Nisku on August 18, 2010
  • Remains discovered in a rural field near Leduc on
    September 1, 2012

Although this list contains all of the unsolved cases still open at the time
of this book's publication, it is unlikely to be a complete list of victims;
Indigenous women and girls continue to disappear from the streets of
Edmonton. Until significant changes are made, it's highly probable this
list will continue to grow.

Anyone with information that might help to solve any of these cases
should contact the RCMP or the Edmonton Police Service.

"In Heaven, Everything Is Fine"

Mitzi Szereto

It's five o'clock on a Southern California winter morning, a Sunday like any other Sunday. The Winchell's Donuts housed in one of the San Gabriel Valley's ubiquitous strip malls isn't busy yet, though the hum of traffic from the nearby freeway indicates that others are already up this hour and on the road. A middle-aged man in markedly poor physical shape, enticed by the fresh-baked donuts and fresh-brewed coffee scenting the cool morning air, decides to pay a visit. Winchell's is a quick walk from his apartment and offers just the cure to counteract his routine state of hangover.

A pair of young Hispanic males in their twenties loiter in the parking lot, seeming to have nothing to do and nowhere to go. The older man takes offense at their presence and what he sees as their aimless existence. He has no patience for slackers. Heated words are exchanged, the first of which are uttered by him. Tempers flare. It quickly evolves into a balletic attack of flailing arms and angry jibes. The fist of one of the younger men makes contact with the older man's head, and he's knocked to the ground. His eyeglasses go flying off the bridge of his nose, skidding along the pavement in a clackety dance that might be comedic if not for the fact he'll now need to get them repaired or replaced.

The scene outside the donut shop is so surreal it could have come from a David Lynch film. In a world where a woman sings inside a radiator and a man speaks backward, nothing is ever what it seems. Why should it be any different for the actor who inhabited such a world?

————————

Marvin John Nance, or Jack Nance as he was more commonly known, was born in Boston, Massachusetts, on December 21, 1943. The eldest of Hoyt and Agnes's three sons, the boy with the twinkling blue eyes grew up in Dallas and would later describe himself as a "Boston Irish Catholic Yankee transplanted to Texas." Nance discovered his *raison d'être* while studying at North Texas State University in the 1960s, and he decided to drop out to devote himself to the acting craft, first joining the Dallas Theater Center, then heading to Los Angeles. He soon moved north, landing an acting gig in a play at San Francisco State University, where he met his future wife, Catherine Coulson (whom he married in 1968). A touring production of *Tom Paine* took him back to LA, but despite offers for acting roles from Hollywood, Nance refused to abandon the play. He returned to San Francisco, and the offers dried up. If he wanted to have a real shot at success, he knew he needed to be in Los Angeles.

Yet Nance's desire for a serious acting career always seemed to be out of his grasp, as he found himself being overlooked for the parts he believed would be the springboard to major success and critical praise, such as the leads in *In Cold Blood* (which went to Robert Blake) and *The Graduate* (which went to Dustin Hoffman), both 1967 releases. However, in the early 1970s, Nance's life would change forever.

Enter iconic film director David Lynch, who was just starting out in his field. Lynch, who was studying at the American Film Institute, was making a film—and he was looking for people to cast in it. The director and actor bonded in typical Lynchian fashion—in a parking lot when Nance noticed a homemade wooden roof rack on a Volkswagen and expressed his admiration for it. Well, not only did the VW happen to belong to Lynch, but he had built the roof rack. This random moment would cement a professional and personal relationship lasting twenty-five years.

The budding young director cast the budding young actor in the lead role of his experimental student film, which later became the 1977 cult classic *Eraserhead*. Undoubtedly one of the most bizarre works of cinema ever made, *Eraserhead* continues to inspire controversy and debate among film buffs and scholars. Taking nearly six years to complete, the film launched David Lynch's career, and it launched Nance's as well. Shot in stark black and white and maintaining a post-apocalyptic sensibility replete with industrial white noise in the background, *Eraserhead* showcases Nance as Henry Spencer, the gloomy misfit with a towering mass of hair whose wife gives birth to a reptilian alien-like "baby" that emits a mewling wail almost as ghastly as its appearance. Henry's sole respite from his horrific domestic existence as main caregiver to the creature is the young woman with a bouffant blonde hairdo and puffy cheeks like scoops of cottage cheese who sings to him from inside a radiator, repeating the cryptic refrain "in heaven, everything is fine."

Eraserhead would end up being Jack Nance's only lead role.

As is common in the profession, Nance experienced the usual routine of feast or famine, with famine often winning out. Perhaps at some point he simply lost heart when it came to landing the major roles and took whatever acting work came his way, supplementing it with odd jobs to pay the bills and using his free time to drink and gamble. Nance was never one to actively chase down parts. David Lynch would later refer to him as a "zero-motivated actor" and has been quoted as saying, "If you wanted him for a film, you'd have to go get him and dust him off." Yet the actor still managed to keep busy, taking minor roles in films including *Johnny Dangerously* (1984), *City Heat* (1984), *Ghoulies* (1984), *Barfly* (1987), *Colors* (1988), *The Blob* (1988), *The Hot Spot* (1990), *Whore* (1991), and David Lynch productions *Dune* (1984), *Blue Velvet* (1986), *Wild at Heart* (1990), and *Lost Highway* (1997), the latter being Nance's final acting role.

In the early 1990s, Nance's career took another interesting turn when he joined David Lynch's noirish television series *Twin Peaks*, playing Pete Martell, the "local yokel" sawmill manager who discovers the murdered body of high school beauty queen Laura Palmer. "She's dead, wrapped in plastic," would become one of the most memorable lines for *Twin Peaks* fans. Pete's character would be reprised in the 1992 prequel feature film *Twin Peaks: Fire Walk with Me*, though Nance's scenes were deleted, only to reappear in the 2014 film *Twin Peaks: The Missing Pieces*. In a further Lynchian connection, Nance's first wife Catherine Coulson, who'd worked as assistant director on *Eraserhead* and was an actor in her own right, played the "Log Lady" in *Twin Peaks* and *Twin Peaks: Fire Walk with Me*.

In the early morning hours of Sunday, December 29, 1996, Jack Nance got into a brawl with two young males outside the Winchell's Donuts located in a strip mall at 438 Fair Oaks Avenue in South Pasadena. Or at least this was the story he told his two friends, screenwriter Leo Bulgarini and his fiancée, actor Catherine Case, with whom he met up later that day. When asked about his blackened eye, Nance reportedly replied, "I told off some kid," admitting he'd got what he deserved, considering how he had behaved toward the two men. Despite being knocked to the ground, Nance still made himself out to be the victor in the altercation. Complaining of a persistent headache, he left the couple and went home.

The next day, Bulgarini went to check up on his friend and found Nance dead on the bathroom floor of his apartment.

Pasadena police and Los Angeles County Sheriff's Department homicide investigators became involved in the investigation. Officers arriving on the scene found Nance's head injuries to be consistent with blunt force trauma. Since Nance had suffered two minor strokes during the eighteen months preceding his death, they initially allowed for the possibility that the actor might have died from a fall. However, in light of the previous day's fight outside the donut shop, they couldn't discount the possibility that Nance might have been murdered. This was given further weight by the medical examiner, who determined that Nance died from a subdural hematoma caused by blunt-force trauma. His toxicology report revealed that his blood-alcohol level at the time of death was 0.24 percent. (Most US states consider an individual legally drunk between 0.08 and 0.10, with 0.40 and higher putting one at risk of coma and sudden death.) Although it wasn't conclusive that either of these factors caused Nance's death, the coroner ruled it a homicide.

Why would Nance enter into an altercation with two men, both of whom were stronger and fitter than he was, not to mention considerably younger—an altercation that resulted in blunt-force injuries to his head? Was he looking to pick a fight? Had he been drinking, or was he already drunk? Those who knew Jack Nance admitted that he could be an abrasive character with a bad temper, and he could also be verbally abusive if someone irritated him. According to the filmmaker who put so much work his way, Nance, by his own admission, said he "wouldn't be too hard to kill" due to his poor physical condition. Were these words a prophecy of his own death?

Nance had struggled with alcoholism for years, acknowledging that it simply wasn't possible for him *not* to drink. Although he did make attempts to kick the booze, he ultimately ended up right back on it again. Aside from his addiction affecting him personally, contributing to the failure of his first marriage (he and Coulson divorced in 1976), it affected him professionally, even as far back as his *Eraserhead* days, when he was told by director Lynch to go sleep it off. Over the years, his drinking continued to get worse. Acting colleagues with whom Nance worked tried to get him help, most notably his *Blue Velvet* costar Dennis Hopper, who stepped in by checking Nance into a California rehabilitation center in 1986. Hopper had been through the same thing himself.

The stint in rehab seemed to do the trick. Nance was back on track, feeling good for the first time in years, not to mention landing more acting roles and keeping his head above water financially. One can only wonder if he might have stayed clean and sober had he not met Kelly Jean Van Dyke, the young woman who would eventually become his second wife—a young woman who was also in rehab for a substance-abuse problem.

Van Dyke was the daughter of actor Jerry Van Dyke and niece of actor Dick Van Dyke, both of whom were considered Hollywood royalty at the time. Despite the family-friendly acting roles she did in her youth, such as appearing alongside her father in episodes of the hit 1960s TV series *My Mother the Car* (a sitcom about a man and his mother, who's been reincarnated as a vintage car), Van Dyke opted to work in the adult-film industry, performing under the name "Nancee Kellie." Her most notorious appearance was in the lesbian porn film *The Coach's Daughter*, undoubtedly a middle-finger salute to her father Jerry, whose successful TV series *Coach* was going strong, even landing him an Emmy nomination. However, rehab was to be Van Dyke's ticket to a new life. In addition to her drug and alcohol addictions, she wanted to put the porn business behind her, not to mention the demons that went back to her childhood. Van Dyke would claim in a 1990 magazine interview (which was never published) that her father had raped her when she was twelve years old and continued to do so whenever he was drunk, even pimping her out to his big-name acting friends, which was why she'd turned to drugs. Though in another magazine interview (published), she admitted to being an alcoholic and sexually active since the age of eleven, and that she just wanted to get her father's attention.

In late spring 1991, Jack Nance and Kelly Jean Van Dyke got married. Nance was convinced he could help her stay clean, but Van Dyke's serious and long-established substance-abuse problem turned out to be more than her new husband had bargained for. Nance himself was trying to stay clean—and being in the presence of someone who was unable to do so was having a negative impact on his sobriety, not to mention being a constant source of torment, as he was forced to watch his wife destroy herself. He decided he needed to get out of the marriage before he ended up right back where he'd been before entering rehab.

Six months after marrying Nance, thirty-three-year-old Van Dyke committed suicide, hanging herself with a nylon cord in the bedroom of her North Hollywood apartment. At the time, Nance was in Bass Lake, California, filming *Meatballs 4*. The couple were speaking on the phone, with Nance attempting to calm his wife, who was threatening suicide after he told her he wished to end their relationship, when a storm knocked out the phone lines. By the time he was able to get help from the Madera County Sheriff's Department, who then contacted the LAPD, it was too late.

Van Dyke's suicide haunted Nance, undoubtedly leaving him with feelings of guilt. Those who knew him say he never recovered from her death. Although he managed to stay sober for two years, he eventually gave up and returned to his previous hard-drinking, self-destructive lifestyle, becoming increasingly disconnected from life and from those around him. Nance's life was on a rapid trajectory downward, and he'd become too broken to stop it. Although he was still able to land roles in TV and film, they were incidental parts. His heavy drinking was wearing thin on directors and others with whom he worked. He ended up being fired from an acting job on the 1996 film *Joyride* after repeatedly showing up on set drunk. That same year, on the final day of a shoot for the TV movie *Little Witches*, he was involved in a major traffic accident involving several vehicles, which left him injured and walking with a cane. Nance found himself right back where he started, living in an inexpensive apartment in an inexpensive neighborhood just as he had done in the early days of his acting career.

Fast forward to Sunday, December 29, 1996.

The police investigation would find no evidence of any altercation outside Winchell's Donuts involving Jack Nance. Nor did they find any evidence of the two men with whom Nance claimed to have been in a fight. They reviewed the strip mall's security footage and interviewed the donut shop's employees, getting nowhere. They had no leads, no witnesses, and no suspects. It was just Nance's story of the attack as told to his two friends, with little to corroborate it beyond the physical injuries the actor had suffered. Even Leo Bulgarini had run into a dead end when he visited Winchell's the night after his afternoon meeting with his friend. Considering that the windows of the donut shop overlooked the parking area, how could a fight at such a quiet hour of the morning have gone unnoticed?

After months of investigation, the police still had no answers, leaving at least one of the officers working the case with doubts that the donut shop altercation had occurred at all. LA County Sheriff's Department homicide detective Jerome "Jerry" Beck had been one of the first to arrive at Nance's apartment, and he quickly realized that the dead man lying on the bathroom floor was none other than the actor of *Eraserhead* fame. Beck, a top-notch investigator with an excellent track record, had a sideline as a technical consultant for television and had even been portrayed by Don Johnson in the 1989 film *Dead Bang*. Yet this case would leave even him shaking his head.

In the Lynchian world he'd made a home in for much of his professional career, is it any wonder that the death of the actor who inhabited this world would be as bizarre and inexplicable as the roles he played? Was Jack Nance the victim of murder by person or persons unknown stemming from a random act of violence? Or was his death the result of an unfortunate accident that took place in his home or elsewhere? If the latter, then this would mean Nance had invented the attack story, perhaps to cover up an embarrassing mishap, the most likely being that he was so inebriated he'd fallen and hit his head. He was already well known among friends, family, and colleagues for his storytelling abilities, which often included embellishing facts, if not making something up outright. Was the Winchell's brawl another of his tall tales?

The symptoms and levels of impairment of a blood alcohol concentration (BAC) of 0.20–0.29 percent are confusion, feeling dazed, and disorientation. The ability to feel pain can change; if an impaired person falls and/or is seriously injured, they might not notice and could be less inclined to do anything about it. Nausea and vomiting are likely to occur and, because the gag reflex will be impaired, this could lead to choking or aspiration on vomit. Since blackouts begin at this BAC, an individual might participate in events they don't remember. Nance's BAC at the time of his death was 0.24 percent.

To add yet more elements to muddy the water, a year prior to his death, Nance told one of his brothers that he had a clot on his brain and had only a year left to live. Then in 2016, Michael J. Anderson, the actor who played the backward-speaking man from *Twin Peaks*, went on a Facebook rant, suggesting that David Lynch might have orchestrated Nance's death. He even threw in accusations that the director was a pedophile who'd sexually abused his own daughter and threatened to kill her if she spoke out (Lynch's daughter has publicly declared the accusations to be untrue). The likelihood of the director suddenly wishing to bump off Jack Nance, a man he said he loved like a brother—a man he felt fated to have worked with for more than two decades—is as surreal as a plotline from one of his films.

Perhaps *Eraserhead* cast a shadow over the actor's life he could never quite get out from under. Not surprisingly, the film has its own share of bizarre deaths attached to it. It was shot primarily at the Greystone Mansion in Beverly Hills, the residence built in 1928 by wealthy oil tycoon and philanthropist Edward L. Doheny (for whom Doheny Drive was named). Doheny gave the place to his son Ned, who, in February 1929, died in a murder-suicide in one of the bedrooms, killed by his friend and assistant Hugh Plunkett, who then took his own life. The circumstances surrounding their deaths remain a mystery to this day. For instance, why weren't the police immediately called? What was the motivation behind the killings—a financial scandal, an illicit homosexual relationship, a salary dispute? Had Plunkett even done the deed? (There were rumors that Ned's wife had been the shooter.) An even closer connection to the film's production occurred in March 1983, when thirty-six-year-old musician and recording artist Peter Scott Ivers, who cowrote "In Heaven (Lady in the Radiator Song)," was bludgeoned to death with a large wooden hammer in his artsy downtown LA "Skid Row" loft apartment. The perpetrator (a burglar? a revenge-seeking colleague, friend, or husband?) has never been caught.

———————

Marvin John "Jack" Nance died in South Pasadena on December 30, 1996, at the age of fifty-three. At the time of his death, he was trying to remake himself as a writer, and had been working on a screenplay with his friend Leo Bulgarini and writing a novel. Despite his alcohol addiction and the tragic personal loss of his second wife, perhaps he hadn't given up on life after all. But sadly, he would never live to complete his new ventures. He was cremated, and his ashes scattered at sea.

David Lynch said, on learning of Nance's death, "I'll miss his dry absurdist humor, his stories, and his friendship. I'll miss all the characters he would have played." In 2002, the director made a documentary film about the man he considered one of his best friends, entitled *I Don't Know Jack*.

As of this writing, Jack Nance's death remains unsolved.

The Railway Child

C L Raven

On September 3, 1939, Britain declared war on Germany. Blackouts, air raid sirens, and the sight of children walking home from school carrying gas masks became normal. Schools regularly held air-raid practices and gas-mask-fitting lessons, and teachers were trained in first aid for gas wounds. Some schools built air raid shelters on the grounds for pupils who lived more than five minutes away, and many schools in Cardiff were welcoming refugees and evacuees. Every inch of newspaper-column space was dedicated to the war. Features about coal prices, names of soldiers missing or dead, rationing, how to make safety clothing, Italy's impartiality, and, of course, Hitler, made headlines. Yet in Wales, the war seemed a distant threat. Until the summer of 1940, people referred to it as the "phony war" and thought the gas masks, blackouts, and evacuations were pointless. (This eerily mirrors people's reactions to COVID-19.) In June 1940, Cardiff would become the first place in Wales to be bombed. But for the Cox family, there was something more dangerous than bombs: men.

Thursday, September 28, 1939, started like any other day under the threat of war. In Whitchurch, a village yet to become a suburb of north Cardiff, Private Arthur James Cox, known to everyone as Jim, was away with his regiment, the 53rd Welsh Signal Squadron. Like many women at that time, his wife Irene stayed home doing unpaid domestic work and looking after their children, Dennis, age seven, and Joyce, four. At 8:30 a.m., after breakfast, Irene said goodbye to them as they left for school. They both attended Whitchurch Infants School on Glan-y-Nant Road, which was 0.7 miles from their house at 50 Heol Don. The Cox family had recently moved from Rhiwbina to Whitchurch, so the children had only been at the school a few months. Every lunchtime, Dennis and Joyce walked home via Ty'n-Y-Pwyll Road, and then Velindre Road, to eat the lunch Irene made. Often, they would call in on their grandmother, who lived on Velindre Road. That day, they were accompanied by their cousin, five-year-old Alan Phillips. However, instead of going home, they detoured to Alan's house at 15 Velindre Road.

The boys arrived there at 12:40 p.m. When Alan's mum, Kathleen, asked where Joyce was, they said she was playing in the garden.

Meanwhile, Irene Cox was growing concerned. Her children should have been home by now. She set out on the five-minute walk to Kathleen's house to see if they were there. Joyce was not. For the next three hours, Irene walked around Whitchurch, visiting different relatives to see if they had seen the girl. Nobody had. Irene next walked to the school, then checked the main road, Penlline Road, in case Joyce had been in an accident. She returned home at three to phone the police.

Dennis admitted that his sister hadn't been playing in the garden at Alan's house. He had last seen her on Velindre Road and assumed she was following them. Since she kept falling behind, he and Alan had continued walking, bored with waiting for her to catch up.

Was someone watching them, waiting for an opportunity to snatch a lone child?

Robert Lewis Thomas, who worked in Heol Don Post Office, said he'd seen her at 12:45 p.m. playing in Lucky Lane, a T-shaped alley that runs behind Heol Don and Velindre Place. One entrance to the alley comes out by number 52—next door to the Cox home. Other children claimed to have seen Joyce in Lucky Lane. If there were other children around, why was it Joyce who was taken? Was it a crime of opportunity because she was alone, or was her abductor targeting her? Whoever took her did it minutes after the children had seen her.

This area of Whitchurch is relatively unchanged since war time, except that, where there used to be allotments, there are houses. The post office is now a residence, number 62; it's famous for being the only house with a red pillar post box in its garden, and the only Edward VIII pillar box in all of Cardiff. (Only 161 pillar boxes were erected during Edward VIII's short reign.) Coincidentally, the person who now owns number 62 is a friend of our cousin.

Joyce was so close to home when she disappeared.

Police organized a two-hundred-person search party consisting of police officers, soldiers, neighbors, Boy Scouts, and Girl Guides. Nowadays, involving children in the search for a missing child would be unthinkable; but with the threat of war everywhere, children were accustomed to fear and death. Joyce's description would have been circulated among the searchers. She was described as plump and of normal growth, with straight, fair hair, and a fair complexion with very rosy cheeks. She had been wearing a blue velvet frock, a navy-blue coat, Scotch-plaid socks, and ankle-strap shoes. She was carrying her gas mask that had her name and address on it.

When darkness fell, there was still no sign of Joyce. The only source of light that evening came from the full moon.

The Blackout had started on September 1, 1939, two days before Britain officially declared war. This meant that streetlights were either dimmed and shielded to point downward, or switched off. Traffic lights and vehicle headlights had special covers to direct their beams downward, and every household had to cover their windows and doors with black, heavy curtains, cardboard, or paint. People were fined for not complying. The *Western Mail* printed articles offering ideas for how families could occupy themselves during the dark hours when they were likely confined to one room (done to avoid turning on too many lights). Every newspaper published daily blackout times alongside reports of people being killed by vehicles during the blackouts. On the day Joyce vanished, the blackout was scheduled for sunset—6:57 p.m.

It was the perfect situation to commit a crime. The perfect cover to abduct a small child. The perfect opportunity to get away with murder.

On September 29, while the rest of Britain's population was being visited by registrars so they could be added to the 1939 Register for identity cards and ration books, police detectives visited Whitchurch Boys' School. The children were all asked the same questions, which were published in the *Western Mail, South Wales Echo,* and *The Cardiff Times*:

"Did you know Joyce Cox?"

"When did you see her last?"

"Where did you see her and what time was it?"

"Did you see her with any man?"

"Has any man recently offered you pennies or sweets?"

"If so, can you describe him?"

A number of children claimed to have seen Joyce on Thursday, the 28th, but no one saw her after one in the afternoon except for seven-year-old Allan Lloyd, who said he saw her later that evening near Coryton Bridge with an "old-looking man" wearing a black suit and a cap. Joyce had her gas mask slung over her shoulder. The boy had never seen the man before. It seems odd that the strange man and Joyce weren't seen by anyone in the search party. A few children claimed that someone had offered them pennies or sweets but couldn't describe him. The age-old urban legend of strange men offering children sweets to lure them away has been told many times. This time, maybe it was true.

Only a week before, the Glamorgan regular and special police forces were alerted about a man who had been seen following young girls. Children were warned to go straight home after school. It's not known whether the police found this man or even if he was the one responsible for Joyce's disappearance. After a brief statement in the newspaper, he wasn't mentioned again.

On Friday, September 29, William Ward, a builder's laborer, joined the search party. He lived two miles away at 22 Queen Street, Tongwynlais; he had a daughter Joyce's age and wanted to help. He was accompanied by his springer spaniel, Jean. They were part of the group searching the disused Coryton railway cutting off Pendwyallt Road, known then as the Great Western Railway embankment.

At 7:30 p.m., Jean pulled William in a different direction from the search party, and he decided to follow her.

The dog led William to Joyce's dead body.

Joyce was lying in the undergrowth on the railway cutting embankment, her head pointing downhill toward the tracks. A tobacco pouch and a copy of the Wednesday, September 27 edition of the *Western Mail* were found nearby. A quotation of some kind was penciled on the newspaper, but police have never disclosed what it was or whether it was relevant to the murder. The newspaper and tobacco pouch may have just been litter thrown away where the killer happened to dump her body, though they were obviously deemed important to the investigation; they are still held as evidence in The National Archives more than eighty years later.

"I had the shock of my life when I saw the huddled body of the girl in a terrible condition," said William.

Private Jim Cox learned of his daughter's disappearance via a telephone call. His unit leader gave him leave. Unfortunately, he arrived home around the time Joyce's body was discovered.

The police immediately set up a cordon and took the risk of using flashlights to aid with photography when documenting the scene. The *South Wales Evening Echo* reported that Chief Constable of Glamorgan Constabulary Joseph Jones (who held the role from 1936 to 1951), Assistant Chief Constable of Glamorgan Superintendent Luke J. Beirne, Superintendent William McDonald, and Detective Inspector Charles Henry Blewden worked through the night, reconstructing the crime. Scientific consultant and lecturer Dr. Wilson Reginald Harrison, who was also the director of the Home Office Forensic Science Laboratories in Cardiff, examined the scene.

Joyce had been sexually assaulted and strangled.

On Saturday, September 30, Professor James M. Webster, head of the Home Office Forensic Science Laboratory, Birmingham, arrived in Cardiff to examine Joyce's body after responding to a police SOS call. Professor Webster had set up the West Midlands Forensic Science Laboratory in the University of Birmingham just before the Second World War started. Joyce's underclothes had been removed. Her gas mask was found that morning, a little farther away from where her body had lain.

There was only a brief mention of her disappearance in the papers—a tiny article on page three swamped by the endless reports of war. More column inches were given to the price of tin than to the "cruel outrage and murder" of a little girl.

On October 2, Joyce's ripped underclothes were discovered in bushes some distance from where her body was found. Had they been torn off at the scene and taken away? The police searched the area extensively in the days following her disappearance, but failed to find the underclothes, which suggests they were discarded after the police had searched the area. Did her killer take them as a memento, and then revisit the scene of the crime to return them, believing the police wouldn't search there twice?

Police believed Joyce was killed elsewhere, then carried to the railway cutting less than a mile from her house. Initially, it was thought she had been abducted by car, as that would explain why no one saw her. But access to the railway cutting could only be reached via a footpath leading to the railway bridge near to where her body was found or by crossing several fields. It's likely only locals knew how to access it. Even today, people struggle to find the entrance if they've never visited there before. Professor Webster said, "In my opinion, one must take four o'clock as the focus on either side of which death might have taken place on the afternoon on which the child disappeared." So where was Joyce in the hours between her abduction and her murder? Did the killer take his time with her, killing her in the safety of his home before disposing of her body in a local beauty spot after the lights went out?

There were workmen on the railway cutting all day on the Thursday she disappeared; if the killer had walked with Joyce along the footpath in the daytime, he would have been spotted.

What made her killer choose that spot? The Northern Meadows lie above the railway cutting, leading down to the Glamorganshire canal. Joyce's body might not have been found so quickly if he'd put her in the canal. Was he disturbed and then panicked, or was the railway cutting more private than the canal?

The cutting is now a nature reserve that runs alongside the council-owned Hollybush Estate and is joined to the Northern Meadows, which come out behind the former Cardiff City Mental Hospital, known locally as Whitchurch Hospital. The railway tracks are no longer there, but the bridges are. We used to be outpatients in Whitchurch Hospital for physiotherapy and breathing therapy in one of the disused wings before the Victorian hospital closed for good in 2016. The hospital is Grade-II listed and heavily guarded to deter urban explorers and trespassers. The railway cutting is one of our favorite places to walk our dogs, Bandit and Romeo, and we're currently fighting the council against building on Cardiff's last remaining meadow.

Police interviewed staff and patients at the hospital. The patients were asked the same questions the children from Whitchurch Boys' School had been. A large number of patients had recently been released from the hospital so it could be used as a military hospital. Eight hundred beds were reserved for wartime casualties, with two hundred remaining for psychiatric patients. Some patients were transferred to other hospitals. In total, police took 1,800 statements from patients, school children, and residents, but no one had seen who had abducted and killed Joyce.

The police unofficially released details of several persons of interest. One man who was seen talking to Joyce was described as having a limp and wearing a black suit and cap. Another was a tall man with a slouch who was "pestering" people on Whitchurch Common less than a mile away. They searched for a "muttering" tramp who'd been seen by a cyclist on Pendwyallt Road, the main road to Merthyr, heading toward Coryton at 1:30 p.m.; he was described as being about fifty-five to sixty years old. Another potential suspect was a retired police officer who was seen at the time by Joyce's aunt, Kathleen, pushing a wheelbarrow with a sack in it. In 1939, there were allotment gardens less than a four-minute walk from the street where Joyce lived; seeing a man with a wheelbarrow wasn't unusual. However, a wheelbarrow would be the ideal method of transporting a body to a location inaccessible by cars.

Another suspect the police were investigating was a young boy. It wasn't revealed who this boy was or why they were investigating him. Though if, as the police believed, Joyce was carried to the railway cutting, a young boy wouldn't be strong enough.

In the September 30 edition of the *South Wales Echo*, Jim Cox said of his daughter: "She was a doll of a girl. Only last Monday I had promised her a present for her birthday and she was full of childish excitement and anticipation. Now this has come. It's terrible." Joyce died only a few days before her fifth birthday.

Her funeral was held on Wednesday, October 4. Women and children lined the funeral route from Joyce's home to St. Mary's Church in Whitchurch; her coffin was carried by four of Jim's colleagues from his regiment. Onlookers stood on graves and tombstones as her coffin was lowered into the ground. Detectives from the Glamorgan Constabulary and uniformed officers were among the mourners. Joyce was laid to rest in an unmarked grave. Since many people couldn't afford tombstones, unmarked graves were commonplace.

During coroner David Rees' summing up at the October 30 inquest, he explained to the seven-man jury that they had to decide whether the person responsible for Joyce's death was guilty of murder or manslaughter. "I hope none of you will make up your minds at all. You and I have a duty to perform—to decide this case simply on the evidence. Anything you read or hear must be discarded from your minds entirely." The inquest was then adjourned for a month.

When it resumed, Rees stated that the evidence proved Joyce had been taken to a house prior to her body being dumped in the railway cutting. Her stomach contents showed she had eaten a meal six to eight hours before death, in addition to the breakfast Irene had given her, and she'd also eaten blackberries. Since she'd had breakfast at 8:30 a.m. and was last seen at 12:45 p.m.—and had died two to four hours on either side of four o'clock—this would probably put her time of death between six and eight. Her mother Irene said that Joyce was not accustomed to wandering about by herself, and she had never failed to come home before. She had also never walked as far as Coryton.

Professor James M. Webster stated that Joyce was a healthy child, though she suffered from a lymphoid tissue condition that would render her susceptible to shock. Her death certificate, which we obtained a copy of, lists her cause of death as "shock and strangulation. Willful murder by a person unknown." She had scratches on her chest and abdomen that occurred two to three days before her death, and abrasions on her left ear and other parts of her body, which were inflicted at or just before the time of death. Abrasions on her neck and other signs indicated manual strangulation.

During the inquest, Irene was given a bundle of clothes and asked if she could identify them. "They were Joyce's," she said, bursting into tears. Her husband Jim crossed the room to comfort her, then helped her out of the courtroom. A thud sounded from outside the courtroom and police officers rushed out to find that Irene had collapsed. An onlooker demanded to know why they had felt it necessary to show Irene the clothes; he was silenced by police officers. The jury returned a verdict of murder by person or persons unknown.

Following the inquest, there were no further mentions of Joyce Cox's murder in any of the newspapers. The media and the locals had moved on, but the Cox family never could.

———————

In 1999, South Wales Police would be one of the first forces in the country to set up a review team for investigating cold cases. They have stated that no unsolved case is ever "closed" and any new information will be investigated. Detective Chief Inspector Mark Kavanagh said that the documents relating to Joyce's case are largely intact, though fragile due to age.

Irene Cox never spoke about the murder, but Joyce's later relatives were brought up to always keep a strict eye on their younger siblings. No one wanted to mention the subject of Joyce's murder in case it upset Irene. Family members said she blocked it out. But as she aged and her mind deteriorated, Irene would talk about a little girl, though she never named her. She died in 2003 and is buried near the entrance of St. Mary's Church in Whitchurch. Her grave slab reads: "Reunited With Joyce, Jim & Dennis."

Even though Joyce died more than eighty years ago, her murder still impacts her family, even those who were born after her death. In 2015, some of Joyce's relatives who were born after her abduction and murder contacted London's Metropolitan Police Service after discovering they had some files on the case that were stored in The National Archives. The Met responded by sealing the records, and in their decision letter they said:

A named subject, who was a suspect, is described derogatorily and should not be associated with these matters. As an unsolved murder, with potential of reinvestigation at any indeterminate stage, practice to close for one hundred years is invoked. However unlikely, indeed remote, it may be that the case is reopened, we have to afford for that possibility. Putting information into the public domain will include naming specific persons who may yet be identified. These persons who may be living may have been witnesses and/or interviewees and who were not prosecuted and who therefore must be regarded as innocent parties. Persons will have given statements in the expectation that their information would not become public knowledge.

The records include fingerprints on a tobacco pouch and the copy of the *Western Mail* with the undisclosed quotation penciled on it. They are sealed until 2040—one hundred years after Joyce's death. The *Daily Express* reported that the records were being kept secret because one of the two main suspects was the retired police officer Kathleen Phillips saw pushing a wheelbarrow containing a large sack. His wife had been away from home that day. Even though the officer had an allotment, there was speculation that Joyce's body was inside the sack. A search of Ancestry.com's 1939 register revealed that there was a retired policeman living in the area—and his home was 0.4 miles away from Heol Don, with the allotments between them. Children were raised to trust police officers, so Joyce would have happily accompanied one back to his house. If he did it, had he been planning to abduct her for some time, and Joyce falling behind her brother Dennis and cousin Alan afforded the perfect opportunity? The officer died in the same decade as one of the suspects.

Terry Phillips, the son of Joyce's cousin Alan, requested information through the Freedom of Information Act. He told reporters that a forensic scientist has told him that advances in DNA technology meant it may be possible to identify Joyce's killer.

In September 2017, the *Daily Mail* announced that Joyce's case was being reexamined by the South Wales Police Specialist Crime Review Unit. Detective Chief Inspector Mark Kavanagh revealed that more than one thousand witness statements had been taken, and there is a similar number of documents and reports. The original investigation by the Glamorgan Constabulary lasted two years and used the Whitchurch police station as its base of operations. (Flats now stand where the station used to be on Bishops Road.) A prime suspect who came to their attention early in the original investigation is still a person of interest today. They also said that a suspect had died decades earlier, possibly in the 1950s—the same decade the retired police officer died. So why won't the Met release the records? Waiting until everyone involved in the case is dead will only protect the killer. They could release the records pertaining to those who didn't ask to be kept anonymous. If they don't decide to reopen the investigation, those who have waited a lifetime for answers will die without ever receiving them. There will be no one left to care.

Joyce's brother Dennis, who died in 2009, never forgave himself for leaving Joyce behind and not realizing she had vanished.

When we emailed the South Wales Police to request information under the Freedom of Information Act, we were told that the case was about to become the subject for a television documentary; therefore, they couldn't release any details.

In June 2021, we received a reply from our Freedom of Information Act request for the fingerprints:

> *Having considered the public interest test we have decided that this information should be withheld. I regret to say this means we cannot make this record open to you or to the public in general.*

*I previously explained that all of the information in the record is covered by **section 31(1)** of the Freedom of Information Act 2000. This exempts information if its disclosure under this Act would prejudice (a) the prevention or detection of crime, (b) the apprehension or prosecution of offenders, (c) the administration of justice.*

A public interest test was conducted with the Metropolitan Police, which outlined the arguments in favor of disclosure, such as providing evidence of how the police investigate serious crime, especially if the victim is perceived to be vulnerable and the crime remains unsolved. Disclosing the information would reassure the public, and it wouldn't prejudice any future investigation or infringe on any individual's rights.

The argument made in favor of nondisclosure was that the record comprises evidence that is key to the unsolved murder—the fingerprints found on the tobacco pouch.

The public interest test concluded that:

In 2018 South Wales Police under whose jurisdiction the murder occurred confirmed that this murder would be subject to a "Cold Case" review and that the information within this record forms part of that process. Therefore disclosure into the public domain of information and material relative to this case would risk prejudicing any line of enquiry that might emerge from this and subsequent reviews. Any action that might risk prejudicing an investigation and prosecution is not in the public interest.

South Wales Police state that following the initial review, the case is to be re-assessed bi-annually. The police continue to retain an active interest in this case.

*The information contained within the Metropolitan Police
service file is relevant to the police investigation into the murder
and may have evidential value in a subsequent prosecution.
South Wales Police have made it clear that it continues to have an
interest in this case, therefore the Metropolitan Police Service has
a duty to ensure that any relevant material remains confidential.*

The record contains information that is covered by the Data Protection Legislation, which prevents personal information from being released if it's at odds with the reason why it was collected, or if releasing it would cause the subject damage or distress. As the record contains sensitive personal information of a number of identified individuals who are assumed to still be living, releasing it into the public domain during their lifetime would be likely to cause them damage or distress and be a breach of the first data protection principle.

In 2040, when the records are due to be released to the public, Joyce's cousins will be in their nineties. The likelihood of police reopening a one-hundred-year-old case by then is highly improbable. They would likely consider it not in the public interest to spend taxpayers' money on a case after everyone involved has died.

Joyce Cox's murder will probably never be solved. Her family will never see justice. Her killer was allowed to remain free until his death. Someone who had abducted, assaulted, and murdered a child—and got away with it—would have felt confident enough to repeat the experience. Was Joyce his first victim? Or his last? How many other little girls lie in unmarked graves, their stories dying with them?

Swallowed Up by the Dark: The Vanishing of Benjamin Bathurst

Ciaran Conliffe

Night fell early in the small town of Perleberg on November 25, 1809. The sun had set just after four o'clock and, with no public lighting, darkness soon embraced the town. Joseph Krause, a courier and guide, was anxious to resume his journey. He was escorting the English diplomat Benjamin Bathurst and his Swiss manservant Nikolaus Hilbert across war-torn Prussia (now part of Germany). The Englishman had been forced to make a swift exit from the Austrian court when Austria signed a peace treaty with Emperor Napoleon Bonaparte, sworn enemy of Britain. Bathurst was a troublesome companion, and Krause was looking forward to delivering him to the coast and being rid of him. Once Benjamin returned from stretching his legs before the journey, they could leave. But he would never return. Neither Krause nor anyone else who knew him saw Benjamin Bathurst again.

Over the centuries since, Benjamin has become a classic example of a mysterious disappearance. As of this writing, at least seventeen science fiction and fantasy stories have talked about Benjamin "vanishing into thin air." The most famous of these is *He Walked Around the Horses*, by Henry Beam Piper. It uses Benjamin's disappearance as the framing device for describing an alternate 1809 in which the American Revolution had failed. The title comes from the writings of Charles Fort, who was largely responsible for making Benjamin a legend.

Fort was an American writer who became famous in 1919 when he published *The Book of the Damned*—a collection of events and things science "could not explain" and which were therefore "damned" and ignored. The book was a breakout hit and became so influential that these are now called "Fortean" phenomena. Fort naturally wrote more books along the same lines; it was in the third (simply called *Lo!*) that he discussed Benjamin Bathurst.

In *Lo!*, Fort argues that there is some unknown cosmic force that teleports people randomly from place to place and perhaps through time or across dimensions as well. He gives examples of mysterious people who came from nowhere (such as "Kaspar Hauser" and "Princess Caraboo") and others who vanished (like the crew of the *Mary Celeste*). Benjamin is one of those who vanished. Fort says: "In the presence of his valet and secretary…he walked around to the other side of the horses. He vanished." That's not quite what happened, but this version of events is still repeated uncritically even today.

Fort gives few other details, though he does mention the account written by Sabine Baring-Gould as his source. Baring-Gould was an Anglican priest and scholar who wrote many novels, as well as books about folklore and history, over the course of a prolific career. This included works on "historical oddities" like Benjamin, though his version was much less sensational than Fort's. Baring-Gould based his article on a book by Tryphena Thistlethwayte, Benjamin's sister. It was mostly a biography of their father, but it's one of our best sources for information about Benjamin's life and how his family perceived his disappearance.

So who was Benjamin Bathurst? He was the third son of Henry Bathurst, the Bishop of Norwich. His father's second cousin (also named Henry Bathurst) was an earl and a cabinet minister. Although Benjamin was not in line for any title or grand inheritance, he was from a good family and had a lot of connections. He attended Oxford (of course) and afterward gravitated to His Majesty's Diplomatic Service, the natural home of well-connected young men with no appetite for the armed forces. The service maintained a pool of young diplomats. As need arose, they were offered postings to various parts of the world. Do well and you could rise to be an ambassador, or use the contacts you made as a springboard into politics. Benjamin's first posting was in 1804—a minor job in the British Embassy in Vienna, Austria. In 1805, he was promoted to a higher position in the embassy in Stockholm, Sweden.

In that year he married Philadelphia Call, who was generally known as "Phillida." Their age gap was unconventional for the time (she was thirty-one, he twenty-one), but her family was upper-class, and later events make it seem that it was a genuine love match. She moved to Stockholm with him, and they had two daughters. In 1808, Benjamin fell ill and the family moved to Cornwall (Phillida's home region) for him to recuperate. (Some reports suggest that this "illness" was a nervous breakdown, which, if true, would be significant for later events.) By the beginning of 1809, he had recovered and went to London to look for a posting.

Europe was in turmoil at the time. Britain's opposition to the French Empire of Napoleon Bonaparte meant there were few countries where British diplomats were welcome. Benjamin's previous experience in Vienna might have been what got him a posting there, since Austria was one of the few countries opposing Emperor Napoleon. Britain was offering a loan to subsidize their war efforts, and Benjamin was sent as a kind of pre-emissary to negotiate this. His job was to tell the Austrians that, if they agreed to the conditions of the loan, then a more senior diplomat (Robert Adair, then serving as ambassador to the nearby Ottoman Empire) would be sent to finalize the agreement.

Benjamin set out from Portsmouth, accompanied by his Swiss valet Nikolaus Hilbert, who spoke both French and German, making him an ideal companion. By the time he reached Vienna on April 16, war between the Austrian and French empires had already begun. This was known as the "War of the Fifth Coalition," one among several in which allied European powers tried to deal with Napoleon. In a previous war, Austria had lost territory to France, and now they hoped to take advantage of Napoleon's war with Portugal to reclaim that territory.

Austria initially seemed to have the advantage, but that didn't last long. Within a couple of weeks, the momentum had shifted to Napoleon, who had taken personal command. He soon invaded Austria in retaliation. As Benjamin arrived, it seemed likely the French could threaten Vienna; the court was preparing to evacuate to Buda (the capital of Hungary, then part of the Austrian Empire), and he was blocked from "presenting himself" to Emperor Francis II because of this. The Austrian emperor did not want to resume full diplomatic ties with Britain in case he had to sue for peace, though he did try to advocate for a British invasion of Europe to draw French forces away. By the middle of May, the government had moved to Buda (and Benjamin with it) while Napoleon occupied Vienna. A surprising Austrian victory in one battle on May 22 did not turn the tide of the war, and, over the next few months, Napoleon ground away at the Austrian forces.

The fighting finally ended with the Treaty of Schönbrunn on October 14, 1809. Austria wasn't completely defeated, but it was the losing side and thus made major territorial concessions. It also had to agree to break off diplomatic connections with Britain. On October 24, Chancellor Klemens von Metternich summoned Benjamin to a private conference. It's likely he officially sent Benjamin home, and unofficially agreed with him to keep a secret connection to Britain open. Benjamin now faced the daunting task of making his way back to England through a continent largely ruled by hostile forces.

This was complicated by the fact that he had no official passport for travel. The treaty between Austria and France included the date by which he was supposed to leave Germany, but von Metternich hadn't asked about travel papers for him. It would take too long to send a messenger to Napoleon to request them, so Benjamin would have to travel without papers. And a foreign diplomat without papers is legally nothing but a spy.

The safest method would have been to head southwest to the Italian port of Trieste, board a boat, and sail through the Adriatic and Mediterranean Seas toward home. Since Benjamin disliked sea travel, he initially decided instead to go north through Prussia (another French client-state), then take a boat from Kolberg (now Kołobrzeg in Poland) to Ystad in neutral Sweden.

Enter Joseph Krause, a courier in the employ of the British government, who had been going back and forth between London and Austria. The last message he brought had been a rebuke of Benjamin for getting too involved in the conflict between Austria and France, something which preyed on his mind. He persuaded Benjamin to head northwest along a route he was used to. They would go to Hamburg, Germany, where they could get a boat directly to England. This was the same route Krause had traveled dozens of times before, and he didn't see any problem with using it.

It did mean going a lot closer to actual French territory, though, where soldiers were known to range out into Prussian territory. This was a journey of seven hundred miles through an unfriendly country, and naturally Benjamin couldn't travel as himself. Even *with* a passport, he'd have risked an overzealous policeman or French officer detaining him. And without one, they'd have legally been entitled to do so. To avoid this, Benjamin became "Herr Koch," a German merchant, though his German was far from fluent. Joseph Krause became "Joseph Fischer." Nikolaus Hilbert traveled under his own name, since there wouldn't be anyone looking for him.

They left Buda on November 10, 1809, in a green four-horse carriage with a retractable hood. The first ten days of the trip were uneventful as they covered the five hundred miles to Berlin, stopping at posthouses to change horses. They traveled at a fast pace, as Benjamin was anxious and didn't want to stop too much to rest. For the same reason, he often walked alongside the carriage rather than sitting inside it, even walking for the entire day. As a result, he was tired and a bit distracted when they arrived at the city. His poor command of German made him think the guards at the gate were going to arrest them. Although this wasn't true, it put him into a state of panic that lasted for the few days they were in the city.

Because the Austrian ambassador was away, Benjamin and Krause visited his second-in-command, who invited them out to a theater to see a play, which Krause hoped would settle Benjamin's nerves. It did not. Benjamin did have some other business in the city and may have had a secret meeting with the Tugendbund, a Prussian nationalist society who were plotting rebellion against the French. He also had a letter from Buda to deliver to George Mills, a former MP who had fled England in disgrace two years earlier to escape his debts. Mills was posing as an American merchant and angling for a position as a British spy. Because of the air of scandal and the coincidence that Mills was the brother of his wife's former fiancé, Benjamin didn't deliver the letter in person.

The three travelers left Berlin in the early morning of November 23, 1809. This was the point in the journey where the paths to Kolberg and Hamburg diverged. With every mile, Benjamin regretted more and more letting Krause chose the route. He had begun to suffer stomach pains in Berlin; by the 24th, they were so bad he spent the night wondering if he had been poisoned. Krause pointed out that they'd eaten the same food, but this didn't convince Benjamin. Privately, Krause remarked to a hotel maid that he was worried Benjamin would die before they reached Hamburg. In the carriage the next day, Benjamin was feverish, accusing Krause of plotting against him one minute, and giving him messages for his wife and his boss at the Foreign Office the next. Then he decided they were being followed and kept expecting French troops to surround them. This was his state of mind when the carriage arrived at its next horse-changing stop: the town of Perleberg.

The original plan was to change horses at the posthouse and keep moving, but Benjamin clearly needed some rest before they set out again. There were no available rooms in town, since it was a Saturday night and there was a ball being held in one of the hotels. All they could hire was a sitting room for the evening in a nearby inn, the White Swan. But Benjamin was unable to settle down. Shortly after sunset, around five o'clock, he went out on his own. There was a detachment of the Prussian army stationed in town, and Benjamin went to call on their commander, Major von Klitzing.

The major had a sore throat, so he had a maid attend their meeting to speak for him. She would later describe the visitor as a "fine young man of distinguished manners," wearing "a diamond brooch, light trousers, and a magnificent fur cloak." She also noticed that he seemed ill, shivering so badly he could barely drink his tea. Even with his poor German and her limited French, he was still able to communicate to von Klitzing that he was worried he was being followed and asked for some guards to escort him back to Berlin. The major realized immediately that "Herr Koch" was no German—he was clearly some foreigner traveling incognito. He refused to give him his escort, though he agreed to have a couple of soldiers go to the inn and stand guard.

Benjamin left disappointed. The maid noticed that he didn't head straight back in the direction of the posthouse, but instead took a side route. Shortly after he left, the son of the postmaster came looking for him, possibly sent by Krause. The maid pointed the young man in the direction Benjamin had gone. By now it would have been fully nighttime; in those days before urban lighting, the streets would have been dark and dangerous. Whether guided by the postmaster's son or on his own, he made it back to the posthouse sometime later.

Benjamin was now fully in the grip of paranoia. He armed himself with two loaded pistols, continuing to rail at Krause. To calm him down, the courier suggested they burn the secret dispatches they were carrying. Backup copies would have been sent by other routes, and the most important details were in Benjamin's head. Without the dispatches, there would be nothing to identify them as British agents. Benjamin was delighted by the idea, and they soon had a merry fire going. He was grateful to Krause for the idea. With his trust restored, he dismissed the two soldiers standing guard with a generous tip.

Now that he had calmed down, Benjamin sat to eat a dinner of turkey washed down with most of a bottle of red wine. After apologizing to Krause for his earlier behavior, he lay on a table for a nap. When he woke up a couple of hours later, it was nine o'clock. He told Krause that he was ready to travel, and the courier went to get the horses sorted out. After sending Hilbert off to help with the packing, Benjamin said that he was going for a short walk to stretch his legs. He left his cloak behind (the evening was mild) but took both of his pistols. Eight people saw him walk down the street, then turn into a side alley. That was the last anyone admitted to seeing Benjamin Bathurst, whether alive or dead, again.

It took about fifteen minutes for the horses to be made ready and for Joseph Krause to start looking for Benjamin. An hour later, and after checking the nearby streets, he went to the ball being held in the nearby hotel to find Major von Klitzing, though he didn't reveal Benjamin's true identity. The major got the local magistrates to organize a search. He also put Krause and Hilbert in "protective custody." Krause later commented on the major's "aristocratic disdain" for him and the valet; they both thought they would have been much more useful helping in the search. Von Klitzing sent some guards to secure their possessions, and they found that Benjamin's fur cloak was missing along with Krause's less expensive one. That was the only discovery his guards made that night.

The next day, von Klitzing ordered the river dragged. He also ordered his men to search the posthouse area to see if the cloaks had been concealed there before setting off to Berlin to consult his superiors. Nothing turned up in the river, though they found the two cloaks hidden in an outhouse. The postmaster's wife and son were charged with the theft, though nothing more, since Benjamin had not been wearing the cloak when he vanished.

Two weeks later, on December 10, Krause and Hilbert were finally released from their "protective custody." They headed to Berlin; from there, they would return to Vienna. In Berlin, they met George Mills, who took advantage of the situation to be the first to send news to London. The Foreign Office found out about the disappearance on December 19. It shows how well-connected Benjamin was that the Foreign Secretary was a friend of his father's and delivered the news to him personally. And, just as Mills had hoped, he was commissioned by the British government to investigate. The Prussian government agreed to cooperate.

George Mills wasn't the only one on the ground investigating the disappearance. John Mordaunt Johnson, a British diplomat and a friend of Benjamin's, took some leave and went to Perleberg to see what he could find out. A German by the name of Rontgen from the free city of Braunschweig was also there, acting as an agent for Benjamin's wife, Phillida. Johnson and Rontgen worked together, but neither they nor Mills could find Benjamin.

By this point, the search had turned up one piece of solid evidence. On December 16, two women out gathering wood found a pair of trousers (or "pantaloons" as they were called at the time) in the woods. They were identified as Benjamin's, and a note to his wife was found in the pocket. It had been written before he disappeared, though it did still offer one important clue. Although it was done in pencil, the writing was unfaded—meaning the trousers had probably not been sitting out in the open since Benjamin vanished. Some accounts say there was a bullet hole in the trousers, yet there was no sign of blood. However, this might not be true. Phillida Bathurst eventually received the trousers, and she mentions neither a bullet hole nor blood in her diary.

This was all further complicated in January 1810, when it became public that a British ambassador had vanished in Prussia. Naturally, the

British newspapers suspected foul play. They printed without evidence that Benjamin had been kidnapped by French soldiers. The French government didn't like that, of course, and they issued a statement that "Mr. Bathurst was deranged in his mind." They also claimed that mental instability was common among the British diplomatic service and that its main purpose was to stir up trouble on the continent. The French view was that Benjamin had run off into the woods and killed himself in a fit of madness, which, like the British view, had zero evidence to back it up. Despite that, these views became established as the public narrative in the two countries.

George Mills privately endorsed the French viewpoint in his report to the British government. He based this on Benjamin's behavior in Berlin, though he seems to have exaggerated parts of it. As a result, the British government decided not to chase up the French and risk diplomatic embarrassment. They offered a large reward for relevant information, then stayed out of it. This turned out to be counterproductive, as many people tried to claim the reward, with most of their stories being pure fabrication that simply confused things. Privately, the British government decided it was most likely that Benjamin had been robbed and murdered, and the body hidden.

Phillida, on the other hand, was firmly convinced her husband was still alive. In March, she paid for a massive search of the area. When that turned up nothing, she decided to travel there herself and investigate. Normally, this would have been impossible (with Britain and France at war), but she had an unexpected "in" with Napoleon. Her younger sister Catherine was the widow of a British admiral who had been friends with Napoleon when they attended the same military academy. The admiral's parents had often invited the poor young Corsican to dinner, and they had become very close. Catherine persuaded her in-laws to write to the emperor, and Napoleon's government provided diplomatic passports for Phillida and her escorts. They left England on June 8, 1810.

Luckily for us, Phillida kept a travel journal, so we can follow the course of her investigations. Their first stop was Berlin, where she received a promise of assistance from the king of Prussia himself, along with authorization to travel to France if needed. The Austrian ambassador also pledged assistance and arranged for Krause and Hilbert to be sent for from Vienna. Phillida then went to Perleberg, where she viewed the spot where the trousers were found. Her theory was that her husband might have camped there, using his trousers as a groundsheet to sleep on. The fact that those in her party were never asked for their passports convinced her that her husband could have easily traveled without one.

When Phillida returned to Berlin, Krause and Hilbert were waiting. Krause, having had several months to consider it, now believed that Benjamin's improved attitude toward him after they burned the secret dispatches had been a ruse. He thought Benjamin might have headed out to try to walk the hundred miles from Perleberg to Hamburg on his own. This would have been a bad idea (it would have been a four days' walk for a healthy man), but Benjamin was not in his right mind at the time. The fact that he asked von Klitzing about getting back to Berlin does make it look as if he intended to leave Krause behind.

If this was what happened, Phillida's only hope was that Benjamin had been picked up by a military patrol. She traveled to the fortress of Magdeburg, which was in the area and where her husband might have been held prisoner, but she found no trace of him. After that, she went south to Paris, arriving on September 2. Napoleon's indulgence had its limits, however, and he refused her an official audience. Instead, she met with the foreign minister. He gave her passports to return to Britain and agreed to place newspaper advertisements stating that her husband "was under the emperor's protection." Having done all she could, Phillida returned home. This was the end of the last search for Benjamin Bathurst.

So, what did happen to Benjamin? The theory promoted in French newspapers—that Benjamin had committed suicide in the woods—is not very likely. Still, he could have, or he could have become even more sick and, as Krause had feared, simply died. The searches probably should have found his body if that was the case, though they might not have. The woods are dark and deep, after all. The one big flaw in all this is that it would mean Benjamin had left his trousers in another patch of woodland (where no body was found) and managed to shelter them so the note in the pocket survived. Although it's possible, especially if he was fevered and irrational, it's not likely.

The trousers also cause problems for the theory that he might have set off walking to Hamburg (or Berlin) and never made it (due to death or capture). Phillida thought her husband could have used them as a groundsheet to sleep on, but he'd still probably have taken them with him (unless he wasn't rational, of course). Phillida's brother, George Call, believed that Benjamin made it all the way to Königsberg on the eastern side of the Baltic Sea, but was then lost, along with the ship he'd hired to take him to Sweden. This was based on the story of a "mysterious Englishman" who tried to contact the British agent in the town. Königsberg would have been well out of Benjamin's expected path, however.

The idea of Benjamin being captured and imprisoned is also unlikely. While he could have been picked up by a patrol in the woods, the chance of a snatch-squad targeting him in Perleberg is slim. Although they could have easily traced him, with Austria now no longer at war with France, his return to Britain would not be a threat. The French would also have no reason to keep his capture secret; in fact, it would have been more embarrassing to Britain to announce it. The only reason it would have been hushed up would be if something had gone wrong and Benjamin had died, either during or shortly after his capture. This is possible, since he was a sick man, but some evidence would have likely emerged afterward.

The most prosaic answer is that he was robbed and murdered in Perleberg, and the killer or killers left the trousers out in the forest as a desperate way to divert attention. Benjamin was dressed in a wealthy manner, after all, with a diamond brooch, expensive clothes, and both gold and silver watch chains. Hilbert also commented that Benjamin was incautious regarding his wealth, exposing the gold in his money purse and his watches. Travelers went missing on the road all the time; it would have been a great temptation to any unscrupulous locals.

The single biggest piece of evidence to support this theory is the discovery of a skeleton found buried in the cellar of a house in Perleberg in 1852. In 1809, the house was owned by Christian Mertens, a serving man at the White Swan Inn. Local rumormongers pointed out that Mertens could not have earned much legitimately from that job, yet he was able to give both his daughters large dowries. The skeleton found in the basement had definitely belonged to someone who was murdered by a blow to the back of the head, and the clothing (the skeleton appeared to be male) had been removed.

The skeleton was the correct height for Benjamin, though the forensic techniques of the day could determine little beyond that. Coincidentally, his sister Tryphena (the one who wrote the book) was in Prussia at the time. She went to view the skeleton, but she didn't think it was Benjamin; the forehead wasn't high enough and the nose didn't seem right. Even if it wasn't him, it still shows that robbing and murdering rich travelers was not unheard of in Perleberg.

One theory is that Christian Mertens had overheard Benjamin complaining about Krause. Seeing an opportunity, he offered to help him get out of town, either to Hamburg or Berlin. This would explain why Benjamin dismissed his guard and apparently left of his own accord. Once he made it to Mertens's house, he was murdered. The pantaloons were placed in the woods by Mertens to divert attention from the town and the secret buried in his basement. Of course, this is all complete speculation. It would need to rely on Mertens managing to sell the diamond brooch and the watches without being caught. There was a sizeable reward for evidence about Benjamin's disappearance, after all.

And then there's the peculiar behavior of Major von Klitzing. Some of his conduct after Benjamin's disappearance seemed designed to frustrate a search rather than help it. He also did his best to avoid getting involved in the investigation afterward. That might have been because he was a member of the Tugendbund, the same secret society Benjamin visited in Berlin. British diplomat Sir John Carey Hall (in a report drawing on confidential Foreign Office sources) suggests von Klitzing murdered Benjamin because he thought he was irrational enough to betray the Tugendbund's secrets. Alternatively, he might have been the one who got Benjamin out of town. There is no evidence for either of these possibilities though, plus the Tugendbund were notorious for being unable to maintain operational security.

Another peculiarity was that when Benjamin left his meeting with von Klitzing, he was heading toward the hotel where the ball was being held. Neville Thompson, who has written about Benjamin's disappearance, suggests that Benjamin might have gone there to recruit a sympathetic noble or one of the drivers to get him out of town. Von Klitzing might even have sent him there. Leaving town in a closed coach he encountered after walking away from Krause would explain why Benjamin wasn't seen departing. It would also mean that he must have met some disaster on the road, either being kidnapped, dying of illness, or being murdered by an unscrupulous driver.

Any of these possibilities could be true, or none of them could. It's easy for us to forget that travel was a risky business in the nineteenth century. Today it takes only eleven hours to get from Budapest to Hamburg by car, a journey you can complete in a single day. In 1809, this was a long and dangerous journey, and every traveler knew they might not reach their destination. Benjamin Bathurst was not the first person to go missing on the perilous path through those dark German woods, and he was not the last. It's unlikely we'll ever know what really happened to him. The woods keep their secrets.

When Boston Turns Its Back

Pamela Costello

Boston is a city known for protecting its own. On June 23, 1996, Karina Holmer's body was found in a dumpster behind an apartment building on Boylston Street. Shockingly, only the top half of Karina's body was found. She was twenty years old, blonde, and beautiful, yet most people in the city do not even remember her name. She is thought of as the nanny who was cut in half. After such a horrific murder, surely someone saw something. However, no suspects were officially named, no crime scene was discovered, and the lower half of her body was never found. How could such a gruesome murder produce no concrete leads or clues? How is it still unsolved twenty-five years later? How could a city so fiercely protective of its residents not yield any results? Karina was a Swedish *au pair* who had come to Boston in search of a better life. She was not a daughter of our great city. She was not one of our own, so it was not Boston's job to protect her.

If you ask the average person on the street what an *au pair* is, they may not know the answer. In fact, the television show *Jeopardy* deemed it difficult enough to include it as a question for contestants. If you ask a Bostonian over the age of forty about an *au pair*, chances are not one, but two crimes come to mind.

An *au pair* is a young foreign person, typically a woman, who helps with childcare and household chores in exchange for room and board. I was seventeen years old in 1996, living in a middle- to upper-class suburb of Boston, and I had never heard of an *au pair*. I knew what a nanny was, yet never knew a family that had one. My family was working class, and I had never been exposed to that lifestyle.

I would find out by watching the evening news that there were hundreds of *au pairs* living in the Boston area in 1996. *Au pairs* appeal to upper-middle-class families because they live with the family and are available during off hours. They are always there to work and can care for children when they are sick, unlike traditional daycare. Additional incentives are that they aren't allowed to work in other jobs, as traditional babysitters and nannies are, and families enjoy the idea of introducing a new culture and language to their children.

Between 1996 and 1997, two horrific murders rocked the city of Boston, both involving *au pairs*. The murder of Karina Holmer happened first. Less than a year later, Louise Woodward, an *au pair* from England, was charged, tried, and convicted for the murder of a child in her care.

Karina Holmer began working as an *au pair* in March 1996 for Frank Rapp and Susan Nichter. She watched their two children, a little boy in the first grade and a younger girl. The family lived in the wealthy town of Dover, located fifteen miles southwest of downtown Boston. Rapp was a successful commercial photographer and Nichter an artist. They had the income to purchase a home with an extra room designated specifically for an *au pair*.

Karina got in touch with the family through a Swedish agency run by Tage Sundin. Rapp and Nichter had previously used Sundin's agency for other *au pairs*, though the exact number of *au pairs* they employed was not known. It's unclear how Karina found Sundin's agency, though he advertised online and in newspapers. One of Karina's sisters had been an *au pair* in England and the United States. Karina wanted to show her parents that she was capable of doing things on her own. She even won a $1,500 lottery ticket that helped fund her trip. It was considered a good omen in the small village where she grew up. Unfortunately for

Karina, before she even left Sweden, circumstances would conspire to make her fateful trip to Boston and her subsequent murder almost impossible to solve.

Tage Sundin, the owner of the agency Karina used, had been convicted and fined by Swedish authorities for not having proper permits. In order for an *au pair* to work in the US, a thirteen-month work visa must be obtained. Since Karina didn't have the proper work visa, she was technically an illegal. It is unknown if she was aware of her status, though it seems unlikely since Sundin had placed at least forty other girls in the Boston area. Illegal *au pairs* are given no formal orientation or instruction. In addition, unlike clients for other, more reputable agencies, Rapp and Nichter did not provide Sundin with a written agreement outlining pay and responsibilities. Karina had no idea what she was getting into the day she left her family and boarded a plane to the United States.

It didn't take long for the young *au pair* to become overwhelmed, and she wrote to friends about the difficult household duties and her high levels of stress. It also didn't take long for the outgoing, attractive girl to make friends with other *au pairs* and go out to explore the city.

Karina spent forty-plus hours a week with Rapp and Nichter's two children. On weekends, she sought out other *au pairs* who wanted to travel around the city and have fun. Rapp let Karina stay at his loft in South Boston on the weekends. He used the loft during the week for his commercial photography business. It became the perfect place for Karina's friends to meet before heading out to their favorite clubs. It was stated that some residents in the building complained about the noise Karina and her friends made, though Rapp later denied those claims.

On Friday, June 21, 1996, Karina and her friends were excited to be celebrating Midsummer, the Summer Solstice. This is a big event in Sweden, with maypoles raised and traditional ring dances performed. It is said the Summer Solstice is a magical time for relationships. However, there would be no magic for Karina on this night.

Karina and her friends left the loft and walked approximately one mile to their favorite club. Zanzibar was a ritzy nightclub located at One Boylston Place, in what was known as "The Alley," across from Boston Common. The Alley, which was closed to street traffic, was the perfect place for young people to congregate when the clubs opened or closed. Zanzibar was known to cater to an international crowd. Karina was wearing shiny black tight-fitting pants, a silver shirt, and was carrying a small backpack purse—an outfit sure to be found in my and every other college-aged girl's closet in the late 1990s. Her shoulder-length blonde hair was pulled back into a bun.

Zanzibar was one of many clubs in The Alley. Karina had no trouble getting in with her fake ID. Though even if she had had trouble, the great thing about The Alley was that, if your fake ID didn't work, you could just go to any of the other nearby clubs and try again. Many bouncers were no match for cute girls. It was easy to get separated from your friends, with so many nightclubs, but everyone ended up back outside in The Alley after the clubs closed.

It was implied that Karina drank heavily in Zanzibar. A waitress even told the media she had her cut off, though it was later suggested that the customer in question might instead have been one of her *au pair* friends. Because many of the *au pairs* looked similar and spoke with foreign accents, this could have prevented accurate testimonials that would help in investigations. It does seem that Karina became separated from her friends. She tried to get back into the club and was turned away, since it was closed.

Around 3:15 in the morning, Karina was seen talking to a man and his dog, both of whom wore matching Superman T-shirts. She was later seen dancing with a panhandler. And then she was gone, never to be seen alive again.

On June 23, 1996, approximately thirty-three hours after Karina was last seen, a man rummaging through a dumpster in the Fenway neighborhood, looking for refundable bottles, stumbled upon a large trash bag. He saw a body part sticking out of the bag and called police.

The upper half of Karina's body was found in two industrial-sized trash bags. Sources close to the investigation said the body was fresh, and even veteran law enforcement officers were disgusted by the scene.

It was determined that Karina's cause of death was strangulation by a rope or cord. It's believed a circular saw was used to cut her body in half. A metal disk that appeared to be from a circular saw was also found in the dumpster. The cut to Karina's body was so precise that investigators believe the killer had detailed knowledge of human anatomy. A partial fingerprint was found on one of the trash bags; it has never been identified. The top half of Karina's body had been bathed, and there were no traces of blood. The dumpster was located behind an apartment building 1.3 miles from Zanzibar.

It is difficult to reconcile the fact that Karina Holmer's killer has never been captured, especially since she was murdered in Boston. Boston is the same city that in 2013 put the country and the world on notice to catch the perpetrators of the Boston Marathon bombings. Police killed one of the suspects; the other fled, and a manhunt followed. The governor asked the public to help find the men responsible for terrorizing the city. He told people to stay indoors, and they happily complied. Public transportation stopped, businesses closed, and even the airspace over the city was restricted. The city and surrounding areas were at an unprecedented standstill. Police searched door to door. The suspect was eventually found hiding in a boat in the backyard of a house in Watertown.

When the Marathon bombing suspect was apprehended, the city was filled with relief and joy. A celebration for police and first responders was held at Fenway Park before a baseball game. The Red Sox players came running out on the field with "Boston" emblazoned on their chests, to the roar and delight of thirty thousand screaming fans and millions watching on television. The victims' faces were displayed on the big screen over center field. David Ortiz, arguably one of the best-known Red Sox players in recent years, took the microphone and reminded the world and Bostonians that this was *our* city, and no one was going to make us afraid.

I remember watching that game and being so proud. Our city was whole again. People had tried to break the spirit of Boston that day, and the city was hit hard, but it was not broken. T-shirts and bumper stickers with the words "Boston Strong" were seen all over the city. I was living in Florida, and I wore my T-shirt with pride. I wanted people to know where I was from, that Boston was my city and that I had the same grit, loyalty, and self-respect as the city I came from. The events of the Boston Marathon bombing attracted Hollywood; two movies and an HBO documentary were made. The movie *Patriots Day* featured a star-studded cast and Boston's native son Mark Wahlberg.

As I get older, I wonder why the city never stopped for Karina the way it did for the Marathon bombing victims. There was grim fascination with her murder, but little outrage. Clubs didn't even close down on the night her body was discovered. Girls were not frantically cutting and dyeing their hair, as they had when the Son of Sam was terrorizing New York. I remember sitting at our kitchen table, looking at the two-page headline in the newspaper. I was curious, though not upset, and I definitely wasn't scared. Karina looked like any other girl in a club.

Perhaps Karina's murder was never solved because it is not the most famous *au pair* case that happened in Boston. Less than a year after Karina was murdered, an *au pair* was charged, tried, and convicted of the murder of a child in her care.

On November 10, 1997, Louise Woodward was found guilty of involuntary manslaughter of eight-month-old Matthew Eappen. Louise was a cherubic-looking nineteen-year-old *au pair* from England. Her arrest, trial, and conviction dominated the news cycle. Karina's murder was no longer front-page news and was rarely mentioned in television newscasts. The Woodward case not only dominated the local news, it became national news. The Woodward case divided the city. You couldn't walk into one of the hundreds of Dunkin' Donuts locations in the Boston area without hearing someone's opinion on it.

I recall watching the news with my parents each night at dinner and feeling uncertain. It was alleged that Matthew Eappen had died due to Louise violently shaking him. I babysat a little girl younger than Matthew at the time, and when I saw the attorney demonstrating the force and the amount of time it would take for a baby to die in that manner, it made my stomach turn.

In spite of this, the case was fraught with doubt. Louise had passed a polygraph test with 95 percent accuracy, asserting that she had not shaken the baby. There were no neck injuries that would have been consistent with shaken-baby syndrome. In addition, a previously undetected, month-old fracture was discovered in Matthew's wrist.

I watched the reading of the verdict for Louise Woodward live on television. Louise was originally found guilty of second-degree murder and sentenced to life in prison, with a minimum of fifteen years to be served. She was visibly upset when the verdict was read and muttered something to her lawyer about only being nineteen years old. I was just two years younger than Louise and in my first year of college, and I was discovering more of the city on my own. At my college, everyone had their beliefs. We were finally adults, and I can remember long conversations and debates taking place in the library and dorm rooms. How could this sweet young girl do something so heinous?

The news reported that alternate jurors were made so irate by the verdict that they threw chairs in the jury room. Louise's sentence was reduced weeks later by the judge to involuntary manslaughter with time served, and she returned to England. Many Bostonians were torn about the outcome; nevertheless, she was convicted and went back to England. There was a sense of closure, and the city could breathe a sigh of relief that she was gone. However, the spectacle of the Woodward trial all but erased any urgency or public help in solving Karina Holmer's murder.

The shock of her murder had worn off. In the Woodward trial, *au pairs* were described as working all week and on weekends, and it was said that they liked to party. Newspapers commented over and over that Karina was out drinking on the night of her murder, and that somehow made a difference.

I had gone out drinking on the majority of weekends since I was fifteen years old. I didn't graduate to bars and clubs until I was eighteen and went to college. Boston is a predominately Irish-Catholic city, and its citizens like to drink. Most twenty-year-olds in Boston went out clubbing and drinking on weekends. Boston is home to many colleges, and everyone had fake IDs.

Newspaper reports framed Karina's actions as reckless when, in fact, they were very common. I frequented some of the same clubs in The Alley. I was never worried, because I was a Boston girl.

Boston girls are no-nonsense and take no crap from anyone; they know how to throw a punch and can walk in heels through a snowstorm. We differed from the out-of-state college kids because bouncers and bartenders could hear our accents and know we were locals. We were protected; bar managers would get us a cab at the end of the night or help us find our friends. On some nights, I lost track of my friends. One disappeared from a club, and we didn't find out until after closing that he had been kicked out and was waiting for us at the 7-Eleven down the street.

We Boston girls had many advantages over our out-of-town counterparts. We knew where to find the closest subway station or, as locals call it, the "T-station." We knew the bus stops, what neighborhoods to avoid, and where the cabs congregated after the clubs and bars closed. We even knew the after-hours places that still served alcohol. We spoke the slang that made it less likely that men would bother us, for fear they might be known to a friend or relative of ours. Even the police were helpful and would never turn down a girl in need.

At that age, you think you are invincible. I survived a couple of close calls, yet I was always out the very next night. Karina's nightlife habits were not unusual. Her lifestyle was the same as thousands of other young adults. It was the same lifestyle my friends and I had, but we were locals.

The residents of Boston are tough, and we take great pride in our city. We hate the Yankees, love the Sox, and worship at the altar of Tom Brady, the former New England Patriots quarterback widely regarded as the greatest quarterback ever to play in the NFL. Most importantly, we protect our families, friends, and our city. I moved away fourteen years ago, but even now say "back home" when talking about the city.

Unfortunately for Karina, she was not from Boston. Like Louise Woodward, she was a foreigner, an outsider. Karina's family was not on the local news every night demanding justice. They were thousands of miles away in Sweden. Back then, the internet was relatively new to most people, and no one was privy to their grief. Karina's friends in Boston were all *au pairs* with no connection to the city. She frequented clubs known to cater to international crowds. The city had no attachment to Karina.

Some reporters and investigators have suggested that Karina was an "unlikely victim." I don't really understand how they came to that conclusion. She was not a resident, she was not a college student, and she was not even an American citizen. She was an illegal *au pair*. How much more perfect a victim could a perpetrator have found? Her family wouldn't be around to look for her, there would be very minimal coordinated search efforts due to possible language barriers with her friends, and she had no affiliations with the city. Maybe some of her friends were also illegal *au pairs* and were afraid of getting caught. After the Woodward trial, the reputation of *au pairs* was damaged, and potential witnesses may have been fearful to come forward. The only thing the killer might not have expected is that Karina's body would be found. If it had not been found by chance, police wouldn't have been looking for a killer. They would have been looking for a missing person.

In the initial days of the investigation, suspects and leads seemed plentiful. Police first focused on her employers, Frank Rapp and Susan Nichter. It was Rapp's loft in South Boston where Karina stayed during the weekends. Police obtained a search warrant for the loft. They collected some items, including clothing that belonged to Karina. In addition, cadaver-sniffing dogs were used.

The search yielded six bags, which were taken into evidence. Police didn't reveal their contents to the public. The strangest thing pertaining to her employers was a dumpster fire at their condo complex in Dover the day after Karina's body was found. Rapp had gotten a permit for use of the dumpster on Saturday, June 22, 1996. Police later concluded that the fire was arson and declined to comment as to whether the fire was connected to the investigation.

Rapp and Nichter were an affluent couple. Rapp was adamant when telling news outlets that he was not a suspect. His wife appeared on a Swedish television show and said the family had been out with her in-laws at a drive-in movie, celebrating her son's last day of school. They both described Karina as a wonderful girl who was loved by their children. Still, questions remain. Who were the other *au pairs* in their employment before Karina? Did the couple know that the agency they continued to use was providing them with illegal *au pairs*? Conflicting reports say they may have employed up to six *au pairs* before Karina. Did they know Karina was unhappy and planning to leave in a little over a month? In the ensuing years after the crime, Rapp and Nichter have declined to be interviewed. The investigation soon moved on from Rapp, and he was never named as a suspect.

Police then began looking for the man with the dog in the matching Superman T-shirts. His name was Herb Witten and he was forty-one years old. He lived in Andover, a city twenty miles north of Boston. He drove to the city on weekends to try to pick up women. Witten was unemployed and had a long history of mental illness; his sister had a restraining order against him.

The sister had acquired the restraining order in May 1996. She said that he kicked her in the foot during an argument in which he claimed that a check from his father's automobile insurance belonged to him. In the affidavit filed with her request for the order, she wrote: "Told us we'd be sorry, that he hates my father, mother and me and that he'd get us if it's the last thing he does."

Witten voluntarily went to be questioned about Karina's murder, then quickly got a lawyer, John Valerio. Valerio said the line of questioning was affecting his client's mental illness. Also, Witten seemed to have a rock-solid alibi; he was pulled over by police for speeding and got a ticket on the morning of June 22, 1996. According to police, Karina would have had to be with him in the car if he was the killer. It was not made public whether police had searched his car when he was given the ticket.

Police outside of Boston are known for pulling over vehicles in the early-morning hours. Driving home from a bar one night, a group of my girlfriends and I were pulled over. We were barely going over the speed limit and we were all sober, but then again, it was four in the morning. We had been out dancing and then gone for breakfast. Going out to breakfast after a night of dancing and drinking probably kept the IHOPs in the suburbs in business.

I remember another time driving home with my boyfriend and getting pulled over after a night in the city. I had been drinking, though my boyfriend had not. The police asked him to get out of the car; however, in both instances, the car was not searched. Routine traffic stops don't usually include a search.

It was widely known that the police did not name Witten as a suspect due to his alibi. He committed suicide less than a year later by slitting his throat. His lawyer believed his client's involvement with Karina's case drove him to suicide. Valerio said Witten had become a shadow of his former self. Neighbors remember being nervous whenever they saw him working with a chainsaw or digging in his backyard. He covered his basement windows with newspapers to further isolate himself. When his suicide was reported, police again reiterated that he was not a suspect.

Witten had documented mental problems for his entire adult life. He was estranged from his family and prone to violence. He had a bizarre run-in with the police a year earlier, when he claimed someone was trying to steal his dog, and he began yelling at cars and taking off his clothes. His best friend was a dog. He lived alone, and he had a basement where his neighbors may not have heard anything. It may be a far-fetched theory that Karina was in the trunk of his car during the traffic stop, and he killed and dismembered her body at home, only to then bring it back to the dumpster in the Fenway neighborhood. On the other hand, to slit one's own throat as a manner of suicide is extreme and uncommon. If he could mutilate his own body, is it too far a reach to think he could have killed Karina?

The next potential suspect was thirty-one-year-old Juan Polo. He was the panhandler Karina was seen dancing with in The Alley after Zanzibar closed. Young, drunken club kids are talkative and generous and there were many panhandlers in The Alley. In 1996, no one used debit cards; everyone used cash. There were hundreds of people exiting the clubs. If a panhandler was friendly, they were more likely to attract kids and money.

Polo had a long rap sheet, with forty-two arrests dating back to 1985. He had been arrested once for rape, though the charges were later dismissed. Polo was questioned in connection with the murder of an ex-girlfriend in April 1995. The police said he had a strong alibi for the murder, and he was never considered a suspect in that crime.

Law enforcement officials concluded he did not have the means to kill Karina.

He was ruled out as a suspect. I cannot help but think that panhandlers know the city of Boston better than anyone. They know remote locations, abandoned buildings, and places where police won't bother them while they sleep. Maybe Juan Polo did have the means to kill Karina?

Over the years, there were other leads in the case that all proved to be dead ends. A musician who lived nearby, was known to collect animal bones, and was heavily involved in the BDSM scene was quickly ruled out. A killer had decapitated two people in a city not far from Boston, yet the modus operandi was much different. He was later tried and convicted for his crimes, and police once again moved on.

Karina's case led police to Florida in 1999 when the severed body of a woman was found in a dumpster. However, this murder was vastly different. Both parts of the woman's body were found, there was a massive amount of blood, and she had been badly beaten. The crime was in stark contrast to Karina, who was strangled and had been washed clean.

Another mystery in Karina's murder is that a timeline of the events and her movements has never been confirmed. Some witnesses came forward in the days and weeks following the crime, saying they saw her a mile away at a Store 24 at the time when she was supposedly in The Alley. It wasn't uncommon for clubgoers to congregate anywhere that was open after the clubs had closed. Another witness claimed he went to Zanzibar with Karina on the night she disappeared and he saw her get into a car with two men. Another witness claimed it was four men. It was also reported that Karina was dating a police officer at the time of or shortly before her death. Although questioned, he was never named as a suspect due to his alibi.

The lack of physical evidence has severely limited the investigation. Police do not know where she was killed. The partial fingerprint left on the trash bag revealed only one of three possible patterns, fewer than the optimum number of identifying characteristics police and prosecutors prefer to have when making a convincing match to a suspect. Police theorized that she might have been cut in half to cover up a sex crime, a pregnancy, or for easier transport, though they did say Karina wasn't pregnant at the time of her murder. There also seems to be a lack of motive.

I am not implying that police didn't do their due diligence and track down every lead. Detective Thomas O'Leary and former chief of the Homicide Unit for the Suffolk County District Attorney's Office David Meier were with the investigation from the very beginning, and the case still confounds and haunts them to this day. They do not go so far as to say it will take a miracle to solve, but they believe they need a major break.

In the city of Boston, there are no memorials to Karina. Her face doesn't appear on the screen at Fenway Park every year with a message asking for help to solve her murder. She is forgotten, only remembered as the nanny who was cut in half, and she was not even a nanny.

Boston did not value or protect her, since she was not one of our own. There was no anger, only disbelief and curiosity because of the way she was murdered. Her life ended suddenly and tragically. Another dumpster sits in the exact spot where the upper half of her body was found. I am as guilty as the rest of the city. I couldn't remember her name. I remembered Louise Woodward's name, but not Karina Holmer's. I remembered the living and not the dead. Louise Woodward's case had an ending. It was a story that could be fictionalized on *Law and Order* and other popular crime shows of the 2000s. Karina's story has no ending; all the unknowns could not be tied up in a bow and explained in an hour. The unknowns still remain twenty-five years later.

Thousands of miles away, her family was sent back half of the girl they loved. In the small farming town of Ålaryd, with a population of less than one hundred, family and friends were left in a state of shock and horror.

Friends knew she wasn't happy as an *au pair* and was planning on returning home in a month. I wonder, did they know the full extent of what she was dealing with? Weeks before her murder, Karina wrote to her friend and former high school classmate, Ulrika Svensson, "Something terrible has happened. I cannot tell you right now what it is. But I will tell you when I get home." What terrible thing happened? Was Karina in trouble? Was it related to her murder? Will anyone ever know?

Was her family, at least initially, spared the gruesome detail that police believe she may have been kept alive for up to twenty-four hours before she was strangled and mutilated? Karina had expressed to her father, Ola Holmer, her doubts about going away when he dropped her at the airport. Ola recalls the last thing she said to him was, "I hope I am doing the right thing." What would have happened to the girl who dreamed of managing or owning her own restaurant? Would she have achieved her goal? Would she have had a family of her own?

As I sit and look back on my life, as I enter middle age at roughly the same time Karina would have, I think about all the amazing things, both good and bad, that have happened in the last twenty-five years. Karina was brutally robbed of her future. But still…no one saw anything concrete or useful?

On July 5, 1996, in a white stone church, a fifty-minute funeral service was held for family and friends of Karina Holmer. Her family wanted to remember her as she was in life: lighthearted and cheery. They refused to wear black. They picked wildflowers to decorate the church. Her coffin was adorned with white roses. The reverend who conducted the service recalls that it was one of the hardest he ever led.

Years later, when Karina's father is contacted for an interview, he comments that her murder is known as an "anniversary," but he thinks of an anniversary as a celebration. There is no celebration in a life cut short. Perhaps the city of Boston will be inspired by Karina's own words from a poem she wrote in 1992, entitled "Life." "The richest gift you ever got is life. Don't throw that away or even step on it. But hold it high in your hands."

Karina's murder may never be solved, but let us not forget her life.

Neighbors at War: The Disappearance of John Favara

David Breakspear

In July 1983, John Favara, a decent family man and hardworking furniture store manager, was officially declared dead—*in absentia*—following an application from his wife.

At ten in the morning on July 29, 1980, Janet Favara placed a missing persons report regarding her husband John with the New York Police Department at the 106th Precinct on 101st Street in Ozone Park.

On the morning of July 28, 1980, John Favara, manager of a Castro Convertibles warehouse on the Jericho Turnpike in New Hyde Park, Long Island, finished his breakfast, picked up his keys, and walked out the door. His wife and their two adopted children would never see him again.

While making the report the next day, Janet told officers that she knew her husband was dead and was waiting for the body to be found.

On March 18, 1980, John Favara finished work, got in his car, and drove home. As he turned onto 157th Avenue in Howard Beach, a bunch of local kids were hanging around a construction site where a home was being renovated. As Favara drove down 157th, a twelve-year-old boy on a Honda minibike rode into the road from behind a dumpster. Favara didn't see him, and his car hit the young boy.

It was a tragic accident.

The young boy's name was Frank. He was one of five children born to Victoria DiGiorgio. Victoria's husband and the children's father was John Joseph Gotti, the future boss of the American Mafia's Gambino crime family.

The Gottis lived at 160-11 85th Street in Howard Beach, Queens. The Favaras lived behind the Gotti home at 160-04 86th Street. The Favaras' son Scott, the eldest of their two adopted children, was friends with John Jr., the oldest of the three Gotti boys, and he would sometimes sleep over at the Gottis.

At the time of the accident, John Joseph Gotti, who later became known as the "Teflon Don," was a *capo* (captain) within the Gambino crime family, the most powerful family within the American Mafia (*La Cosa Nostra*). Through the 1960s and '70s, the Gambino family became a Mafia powerhouse under the leadership of its namesake, Carlo Gambino. In January 1986, Gotti was declared the family's official boss, a position he took for himself after ordering the infamous murder of the prior family boss, Paul Castellano. Castellano and Thomas Bilotti, his driver/bodyguard and underboss of the Gambino family, were gunned down at 5:26 p.m. on December 16, 1985, outside Sparks Steak House on East 46th Street in Midtown Manhattan.

By the time Gotti seized control, the Gambino crime family had an income of more than $500 million a year.

Frank Gotti's older brother, also named John (following the Italian tradition of naming the firstborn male after the paternal grandfather), was the former acting boss of the Gambino family, from 1993 to 1999. In a 2010 interview with Steve Kroft for *60 Minutes Presents*, he was asked if he believed his father was involved in the disappearance of Favara. John Jr. replied, "Knowing John, and how he was, and how he felt about a lot of things, especially regarding his own children, he probably was. Do I know with certainty? No! He never discussed it with me."

Young Frank's dreams were dashed when he didn't make the cut for the school's football team. However, John Gotti paid his son's football coach a visit, after which the coach had a change of mind. On March 19, 1980, Frank was due to attend his first football practice session with his new teammates.

Sadly, it was never to be.

In the late afternoon of March 18, 1980, Frank was playing outside with some boys from his neighborhood when he asked for a turn on his friend Kevin McMahon's minibike. Frank and the others were riding it on a construction site near the side of the road, a few blocks away from the Gotti family home.

Frank's mom, Victoria, was in the kitchen preparing dinner when the house phone rang. Frank's sister, also named Victoria, answered. It was their neighbor and family friend, Marie Lucisano, calling to tell them that Frank had been in an accident. As soon as the younger Victoria told her mom what had happened, the elder Victoria rushed to the scene. When she arrived, an ambulance was already there. It did not look good. Frank was taken to the trauma unit of the local hospital, but by then it was too late.

Hospital officials phoned John, who was in a meeting at his headquarters, the Bergin Hunt and Fish Club on 101st Avenue in Ozone Park. (The Club would later become the Gambino family headquarters after Gotti was declared boss.) In later years, his son John Jr. has spoken about hearing his father through the air duct at home, crying alone in his den after returning from the hospital.

It was at the hospital that John had to tell his wife the tragic news. John Jr. has also publicly discussed how his father was scared for the first time in his life when he saw Victoria sitting in the waiting room, still unaware of her son's death, and having to pluck up the courage to tell his wife the news he knew would break her heart.

Not long after Frank's death, Victoria, who was struggling to come to terms with her young son's death and the circumstances surrounding it, smashed a mirror and tried to cut herself with the broken pieces. She also attempted to end her life by taking an overdose of pills she'd been prescribed. Gotti rushed to his wife's aid, carrying her in his arms to their doctor's private residence. She survived after having her stomach pumped.

John Favara was devastated at being involved in such a tragic accident. But others, especially the Gottis, saw it differently. Two days later, an anonymous female telephoned the NYPD's local precinct, declaring, "The driver of the car that killed Frank Gotti will be eliminated." Although Favara was warned of this by the police, he brushed it off. In the following days and weeks, Favara continued to receive death threats. A mass card from Frank's funeral, along with a photo of young Frank, was placed in the Favaras' mailbox. Favara's car was also stolen; when it was returned on May 22, it had "MURDERER" spraypainted on the sides.

Favara approached his friend Anthony Zappi for advice. Zappi told him to sell his car, sell his house, and move away from the area. (Zappi's father Ettore, who died at his Florida home in 1986 at age eighty-two, had been a *capo* in the Gambino family.) Other friends had previously warned Favara that he should either get a gun to kill John Gotti or sell up and move away. Favara was aware of Gotti's rising status within the family.

FBI files show that Ettore Zappi's home, on Club Drive in Massapequa, Long Island, had been under surveillance for a number of years. John Favara is listed as having visited the Zappi home numerous times between March 8 and March 28, 1968; June 3 and June 9, 1972; July 21 and July 27, 1973; and August 4 and August 10, 1973. However, it was accepted that Favara was not a person of interest to law enforcement agencies.

After he was attacked in his driveway on May 28, 1980, by Frank's mother Victoria wielding a baseball bat, Favara decided enough was enough. The Favaras put their house up for sale, and a sale was subsequently due to go through on July 29—the same day Janet reported her husband missing.

On July 25, 1980, three days before John Favara disappeared, John Joseph Gotti took his wife on a much-needed vacation to Florida. They returned to New York on the fourth of August, and both were interviewed over Favara's disappearance. Victoria told detectives, "I don't know what happened to him, but I'm not sorry if something did. He never sent me a card. He never apologized. He never even got his car fixed." John merely shrugged, saying, "He killed my kid."

On August 5, 1980, William Battista, a long-time FBI informant and Gambino associate, and a regular visitor to the Bergin Hunt and Fish Club, reported that Favara's body would never be found. According to another informant, Gotti had not initially planned to take revenge. However, he was told that Favara was drunk and had been speeding, jumping a stop sign. The informant went on to say that Gotti then changed his mind.

Following Janet's July 29, 1980, police report, the investigation into her husband's disappearance took the NYPD to Nassau County, where it was picked up by the intelligence unit of the Nassau County Police Department.

John Favara was last seen on July 28, 1980, walking toward his car at approximately 4:50 p.m. He had parked in his usual spot at the rear of the Capitol Diner. The diner, where Favara ate lunch regularly, was next door to Castro Convertibles. Favara had been a highly respected and trusted employee at the dealership for thirteen years prior to his disappearance. During a search of the area where he was last seen, several items of interest were discovered: one rust-colored button with rust-colored thread still attached, two white buttons, and, worryingly, two spent .22 shell casings. Janet Favara reported that, when she had last seen

John, he was wearing rust-colored pants and a light-colored sports shirt. Eyewitnesses described seeing three White men assaulting a White male. The individual, considered to be John Favara, was being attacked by two of the men, who beat him with two-by-fours before shooting him and bundling him into the back of a blue van. The van then took off with its tires squealing, immediately followed by a four-door green sedan. The van had left a skid mark on the pavement. Investigators found a talon pants-clip with white thread attached. Nearby were four beer bottles sitting on a wall. Favara's car had also disappeared from its parking spot.

In a September 23, 1980, US government memorandum from a special agent located in Garden City, Long Island, it was stated that the investigation into the possible kidnapping and murder of John Favara had failed to identify any suspects and recommended that the case be closed.

American journalist and author Gerald "Jerry" Capeci, considered by CNN and the BBC to be an expert on the American Mafia, published a story on March 8, 2001, regarding the abduction of Favara. Capeci put the story together using information from former and current law enforcement contacts. In his article, Capeci names an eight-man crew he believes participated in the abduction, murder, and disappearance of Favara: the Carneglia brothers, Charles and John; Angelo Ruggiero; John Gotti's brother Gene; and Willie Johnson, Iggy Alogna, Richard Gomes, and Anthony Rampino, all of whom were linked to the Gambino family. More specifically, they were all linked to John Gotti.

Capeci writes: "As Favara approached his automobile, he spotted the men and turned to run. John Carneglia dropped him with two shots from a .22 caliber, silencer-equipped pistol. Favara gasped, 'No. No. Please, my wife.' As he struggled to get off the ground, Gomes—a former hood from Providence, Rhode Island, who had joined the Gotti crew in the late 1970s—cracked Favara over the head with a two-by-four, picked him up and threw him in a van. Another crew member took the victim's keys and followed in Favara's car. Favara and his car were driven to a salvage yard in East New York operated by the Carneglias. Favara's body was stuffed into a barrel. Charles Carneglia disposed of the barrel in the ocean off Brooklyn; his brother John crushed Favara's car at their salvage yard."

In 2004, the FBI were informed by former-Bonanno-crime-boss-turned-government-witness Joseph Massino that he believed Favara's remains were buried on the Brooklyn-Queens border, in a parking lot suspected to be a Mob graveyard favored by the Gambino family. On October 4, 2004, the FBI began excavating the site, and a week later found the remains of two bodies. FBI agents also found a Citibank card belonging to a *capo* from the Bonanno crime family, Dominick Trinchera, and a Piaget wristwatch, which, upon further investigation, was confirmed as belonging to another Bonanno *capo*, Philip Giaccone. Trinchera and Giaccone were murdered, along with a fellow *capo* of the Bonannos', Alphonse Indelicato, a.k.a. "Sonny Red," on May 5, 1981, for conspiring to overthrow the boss of the Bonanno family, Philip Rastelli.

The murders of Indelicato, Trinchera, and Giaccone (who thought they were there to talk about a peace agreement) took place at the 20/20 Night Club in Clinton Hill, Brooklyn, and were carried out by Massino's brother-in-law Salvatore Vitale and three others. The assassins, all wearing ski masks, had hidden in a closet at the club. One of the assassins was Canadian mobster Vito Rizzuto.

Sal Vitale, a former underboss as well as government witness, said several members of the Gambinos, two of whom he claimed were John Carneglia and John Gotti's brother Gene, buried the bodies. But in May 1981, at the same parking lot, only the body of Indelicato had been discovered.

The FBI did not find any evidence of John Favara having been buried at the parking lot.

Philip Rastelli was declared boss of the Bonanno family during a meeting of the Commission at the Americana Hotel in Manhattan on February 23, 1974. He remained boss until his death on June 24, 1991, at which time Joseph Massino became boss. During his time as boss, Rastelli spent all but two years of his reign in prison.

On February 7, 2008, a planned takedown of the Gambino family by law enforcement agencies across New York saw more than sixty alleged Mafia members and associates arrested, one of whom was Charles Carneglia. Another was Kevin McMahon. In 1979, Charles Carneglia and his brother John had taken Kevin in as a homeless twelve-year-old boy (his parents were drug addicts, and his mother had murdered his father).

On January 6, 2009, Assistant US Attorneys Roger Burlingame, Marisa Megur Seifan, and Evan M. Norris filed a forty-four-page motion against Charles Carneglia that included additional information from an informant on the Favara case. One of the uncharged crimes listed was the disappearance and alleged murder of John Favara. "In 1980, upon the direction of Gambino family soldier Angelo Ruggiero, the defendant disposed of the body of John Favara. John Gotti Sr., a powerful Gambino captain at the time and the future boss, ordered Favara's murder because Favara accidentally struck and killed Gotti Sr.'s son when the boy darted into traffic riding a dirt bike he had borrowed from CW2 [McMahon]."

The opening paragraph to the motion said: "The government submits this motion in limine [referring to a motion before a trial begins] to admit certain evidence at trial of uncharged crimes and other acts committed by the defendant. As set forth below, the evidence is admissible as direct proof of the structure and organization of the charged racketeering enterprise, the defendant's membership, and on-going participation in the enterprise's illegal activities for over thirty years, and the existence, nature and continuity of the charged racketeering conspiracy."

The prosecutor's motion went on to explain: "The defendant [Carneglia] told Gambino family associates [McMahon] and CW3 [Peter Zuccaro, a former enforcer for the Gambino family] he disposed of bodies for the Gambino family and told [McMahon] he disposed of Favara's body by placing it in a barrel of acid. In a later discussion concerning his expertise at disposing of bodies for the Gambino family, which included a discussion of a book the defendant was reading on dismemberment, the defendant informed Gambino family associate CW1 [John Alite] acid was the best method to use to avoid detection. Years later, the defendant asked [McMahon] to help him move barrels of acid in his basement and alluded to the fact the barrels had been used in connection with disposing of a number of bodies, which [McMahon] understood to be a key component of the defendant's value to the Gambino family."

Kevin Graham, a staff writer for the *St. Petersburg Times*, reported on December 11, 2008: "According to the US Attorney's Office, Alite has acknowledged his role as a top associate in the crime family and specifically admitted to participating in the murder of George Grosso on Dec. 20, 1998, and in the murder of Bruce John Gotterup on Nov. 20, 1991 [two murders linking Alite to John Angelo Gotti]." Prosecutors said Alite also admitted to participating in four murder conspiracies, including conspiracy to kill Louis DiBono in 1990 (a murder linking Alite to Charles Carneglia and Kevin McMahon).

John Alite claimed in his evidence that he'd been secretly seeing Victoria Gotti, prompting Victoria to say to reporters, "He's an insect. He would hump a cockroach." On December 10, 2008, John Alite pleaded guilty to RICO (Racketeer Influenced and Corrupt Organizations Act) charges linking him to John Gotti's eldest son, John Angelo Gotti. Alite, who previously pleaded guilty to the RICO indictment at a hearing in January 2008, agreed to testify on behalf of the government. However, this was kept secret and only announced in December 2008 because Alite was due to provide evidence in another RICO case. In 2011, Alite was sentenced to ten years' imprisonment, but due to his testifying for the government, he was released from prison in 2012 on a five-year supervised release.

McMahon had also been charged with several serious crimes, including being implicated in two murders he admitted to—Carneglia was the only one who took his chances at trial—and at the time of Carneglia's trial, McMahon was awaiting sentence. He repaid the Carneglias for taking him in when he was a homeless young boy by flipping and turning against his former guardians to save his own neck. McMahon was facing a life sentence for his crimes; however, his reward for becoming a government witness was time served. By the time he received his sentence, this amounted to less than five years. McMahon identified Carneglia as the man who disposed of Favara by dissolving his body in a barrel filled with acid. As stated above, McMahon told authorities he and another individual were told by Carneglia that acid was "the best method to use to avoid detection."

"In 1980, upon the direction of Gambino family soldier Angelo Ruggiero, the defendant disposed of the body of John Favara. John Gotti, a powerful Gambino captain at the time, ordered Favara's murder because Favara accidentally struck and killed Gotti's son when the boy darted into traffic riding a dirt bike that he had borrowed from CW2 [McMahon]." Kevin McMahon also stated that Carneglia had informed him that, because McMahon owned the minibike Frank Gotti was riding in the accident that killed him, he (Carneglia) had protected McMahon from retaliation by John Gotti.

Assistant US Attorney Roger Burlingame said McMahon's cooperation was exceptionally brave. "The truly horrific thing about the Carneglias is the manipulation of a thirteen-year-old who had been rejected and betrayed at every turn, and they saw that as an opportunity for a flunky who would run through walls for them, a henchman at their disposal."

McMahon didn't speak in open court. But in a letter to and read out by the judge, he wrote: "I truly believe John Carneglia saved my life," before going on to write: "My biggest mistake was when John Carneglia went to prison in June 1989 I should have moved away.

Instead, I felt obligated to John and his family, and I became closer to Charles Carneglia. This is how I got involved in these heinous crimes, which I sincerely regret."

Kevin McMahon, an Irish gangster who was unofficially adopted by the Carneglias at the age of twelve and was aware of the brothers' murkiest secrets, eventually took the witness stand on February 17, 2009.

Information McMahon gave prosecutors included that Carneglia had used the wrong acid in disposing of Favara's body, which was taking longer than expected to dissolve. McMahon went on to state that Angelo Ruggiero had reprimanded Carneglia, who then changed the acid, and eventually the body was dissolved. To prove he'd completed the job, Carneglia is alleged to have then gone to the Lindenwood Diner in Howard Beach, where Ruggiero was at a table eating. Carneglia walked up to Ruggiero and casually tossed finger bones belonging to the deceased Favara into a bowl of chicken soup Ruggiero was enjoying.

McMahon admitted he was breaking a fundamental Mob rule when he said, "Don't rat—that's always a good one." A similar quote was made during Alite's testimony. "Don't do what I'm doing: ratting."

The Carneglias treated McMahon like one of their own. John was his "adopted" father, and Charles his "crazy uncle." On May 23, 1989, John Carneglia was convicted of running a heroin distribution ring (he was convicted along with Angelo Ruggiero and Gene Gotti). On July 7, 1989, Carneglia was sentenced to fifty years in prison. John Carneglia, Bureau of Prisons registration number 04196-016, would be released from prison on June 11, 2018.

McMahon explained that when John Carneglia was sent to prison, it was a "bad day" for him. Carneglia had previously warned McMahon to stay away from his brother Charles. However, after he was sent to prison, Charles took McMahon under his wing. McMahon said that when Carneglia went to prison, "it was like losing a father." McMahon told prosecutors he believed John Gotti didn't like him. But all that changed in 1986, when McMahon played a significant role in Gotti's acquittal.

After that, Gotti considered McMahon a lucky charm and would even take him to card games. "He said I brought him luck," stated McMahon.

Following the imprisonment of John Carneglia, Charles put McMahon to work. McMahon admitted he'd participated in the 1990 killings of Gambino soldier Louis DiBono and armored-car guard Jose Delgado Rivera. McMahon claimed he was given a diamond bracelet worth $10,000 for the DiBono murder.

On Tuesday, March 17, 2009, following a six-week trial, a federal jury convicted Charles Carneglia. Senior US District Judge Jack B. Weinstein sentenced him "to life imprisonment for RICO conspiracy, including predicate acts of murder, murder conspiracy, felony murder, robbery, kidnaping, marijuana distribution conspiracy, securities fraud conspiracy, and extortion."

Assistant US Attorney Roger Burlingame said, "The defendant has led a profane life, his sole role in the Gambino family was to kill and dispose of bodies," adding, "He relished the job. He desecrated the bodies of Gambino family victims by melting them in acid."

The four murders for which Carneglia was found guilty began with the 1977 murder of Gambino family associate Michael Cotillo; followed by the 1983 murder of Salvatore Puma, another Gambino family associate; the 1990 murder of Gambino family soldier Louis DiBono; and the 1990 felony murder of Jose Delgado Rivera, the armored-truck driver Carneglia and others (including McMahon) murdered during a robbery at JFK Airport.

During the sentencing hearing, Carneglia, who was slouched in his chair, sneered as relatives of his victims read out their impact statements. One said, "Charles Carneglia, you have no soul; there is a darkness that surrounds you every day. [...] My brother would ask to show you mercy, but I am not my brother. I ask that they lock you up in a cage fitting for the animal you are. A filthy sewer where vermin like you belong."

Carneglia then had his chance to address the court and said, "Liar after liar testified against me and they all had cooperation agreements."

No one has yet been brought to justice over the disappearance of John Favara, and his body has still not been recovered.

The Pype Hayes Murders

Paul Williams

I grew up in Erdington, a suburb of Birmingham, in the 1970s and 1980s. Ignoring claims from Manchester, Birmingham is the second largest city in the United Kingdom. One of its largest parks is Pype Hayes Park, which starts at Erdington's northern boundary. An oasis of greenery in a gray industrial city, the park covers one hundred acres, extending from an old manor house into the suburb of Walmley. The next place after Walmley is Sutton Coldfield, formerly a royal town. In my time, aspiring middle-class people from Erdington migrated to Sutton Coldfield, which was then regarded as more affluent.

Pype Hayes Park formed an unofficial line between Erdington and Sutton Coldfield, contrasting beautiful gardens, fishing ponds, and tennis courts with teenagers taking illicit drugs, drinking cheap alcohol, and having sex in the bushes. A circus camped there annually, and an extravagant display of fireworks on November 5, Guy Fawkes Night, attracted crowds from across the city. The park, which is surrounded by estates with council housing, has its main entrance on the busy Chester Road, which leads to intersections that connect the city center about five and a half miles away with motorways that go to the north and south of England.

The area around Pype Hayes Park was the scene of two unsolved murders, one at the Erdington end of the park and the other closer to Walmley. Both victims were twenty-year-old women. Both died on May 27 at the end of the Whitsunday weekend after attending a dance. Both appeared to have been raped. One was strangled and left in a ditch, the other drowned in a pit. In both cases, the only suspect was a man named Thornton who was charged and acquitted. Despite these apparent similarities, it is impossible that the two women were killed by the same person, since they were separated by 157 years.

Barbara Forrest moved from Corby in Northamptonshire to Erdington in early 1974. She was five feet, six inches tall, with long dark hair and a fresh complexion. She worked at a residential children's home, Pype Hayes Hall, which had been converted from the manor house in the late 1940s. It housed a maximum of thirty-five children who had been placed in council care up to the age of fifteen. After a boy was killed by his foster parents in 1948, residential homes were increasingly used by councils. At the same time, the policy of sending children overseas ended, and the wartime evacuation program was reassessed. There were approximately 2,435 children in council care across Birmingham in 1974, with more homes for them under construction.

Barbara's boyfriend Simon Belcher, the son of a pastor, lived on the other side of Birmingham. The couple had been dating for five years and regularly attended church services at St. Mark's Lutheran Church in the city center.

On Monday, May 27, a public holiday, Simon and Barbara went to a disco called Knickers on Soho Road in the suburb of Handsworth, then traveled back into Birmingham city center. After they kissed goodnight, Barbara said she could get home by herself. Simon gave her change for the bus, since the West Midlands public transport system required exact fare in coins. He left her at the bus stop in Colmore Circus after she had confirmed with a waiting stranger that the number 67 bus had not yet departed. It is a route I have traveled on many times, passing through Aston and along Tyburn Road toward Castle Vale, which had a reputation as the area's roughest housing estate. Barbara's ride home would have taken about twenty minutes. The best place for her to disembark was outside the Bagot Arms public house; from here she would have a five to ten minutes' walk back to the junction and along

Chester Road by the park to the hall. Alternatively, she could have alighted at the previous stop and avoided walking past the Bagot Arms. Simon is the last person known to have seen her alive.

We cannot be certain Barbara was on the bus, which left Colmore Circus on time at one o'clock. The driver, Harold Watts, remembered her face, but was unsure if she traveled that night. None of the other passengers, including three who boarded at the stop where she parted company with Simon, remembered her. No one waiting for other buses in the area came forward to say they had seen Barbara either. This is perhaps unsurprising, as most people going home from the city had spent the last night of the holiday weekend drinking heavily. The stranger she spoke to was described by Simon as five feet, eleven inches tall, and about forty-five years old. He was dressed smartly and soberly.

Searchers began looking for her the next day. A week later, on June 4, Barbara's naked body was found in a ditch in Pype Hayes Park, about seven and a half yards from Chester Road and three yards from a path leading to prefabricated buildings between the road and the park. She had been raped. The police questioned Simon Belcher for several hours, accepting that he had returned home after leaving Barbara. He told them she was not promiscuous, though he was aware of other men in her life, the most recent being a married man. That experience had deterred her from other sexual relationships. None of the men were still associated with her, and Simon did not know of anyone who might wish her harm.

A policewoman, Lynda Maddison, wearing a blue evening dress and turquoise coat like Barbara's, staged a reconstruction of the victim's last known movements on the following Monday. It was unsuccessful due to there being fewer people about on a regular weekday than on a bank holiday. The reconstruction was publicized in local newspapers and on television. The questioning of taxi drivers revealed that two girls had taken a taxi from the city to the Bagot Arms at 12:40 a.m. on the night of Barbara's disappearance. One walked toward Walmley, and it was thought she might have seen a suspicious man hanging around. After the Bagot Arms closed for the evening, there was no reason for anyone to be waiting in the area. Neither girl contacted the police.

Investigations continued. Posters requesting information were attached to lampposts and trees around Erdington and Walmley. In July, the police drained the lake in Pype Hayes Park, relocating fish, much to the annoyance of local fishermen, and looking for unspecified clues. Nothing was discovered. In September, a colleague of Barbara's was arrested on suspicion of her murder. Michael Ian Thornton was employed as the deputy superintendent at Pype Hayes Hall. Aged thirty-six, he came from Lytham St. Annes in Lancashire and, like Barbara, lived on-site. He was remanded by the magistrates fifteen times before the case was sent for trial at Birmingham Crown Court. It was eventually heard in March 1975.

The prosecution claimed Thornton killed Barbara in a moment of passion. The evidence was circumstantial. Thornton allegedly asked his mother to say he was at home on the night Barbara disappeared. He had small spots of blood on his trousers, which had been dry-cleaned. It was impossible to identify the blood as human or animal. On the night before the murder, Thornton visited his friend Henry Stokes in London; he went for a drink with him and then drove back in the direction of Birmingham. No one saw him arrive. Stokes testified that Thornton was not a violent man.

Albert Clayton, who discovered the body, was accused by the defense lawyers of knowing it was there several days earlier. He denied this, and the witnesses he approached following the discovery said his actions appeared genuine. Albert walked his dog along the path daily, as did others. The area was also searched extensively by people looking for Barbara. It is hard to believe her body lay there undiscovered for a week, which raises the possibility that someone had hidden it elsewhere, such as in the accommodation at the hall used by Thornton. For this reason, the charge against him did not specify the exact date of the crime.

Thornton was acquitted due to lack of evidence. No one could place him in the area, and his trousers weren't examined until his arrest four months after the murder, so it was impossible to prove where and when the bloodstains were made. There were no further arrests, and the case was largely forgotten. In November 1974, explosions at city center pubs by the IRA in Birmingham killed twenty-one people. Six men were convicted the following year, then released in 1991 when some of the evidence against them was found to have been fabricated by the police.

At the time of Barbara's disappearance, the police said they were studying similarities with the disappearance of two other girls who had vanished at bus stops in the Midlands: twenty-one-year-old Lucy Partington from Cheltenham and seventeen-year-old Carolyn Allen from Nottinghamshire. Lucy, a cousin of the novelist Martin Amis, was abducted in Cheltenham in 1973, and later found to be a victim of the notorious serial killers Fred and Rosemary West. Carolyn disappeared on April 10, 1974, intending to travel from Bramcote to her home in Kinoulton. Her body was found in woodlands in Leicestershire in December 1975. She had been beaten around the head and her jeans were missing, but it was not possible to ascertain the cause of death. Some researchers have suggested she was a victim of the "Yorkshire Ripper" Peter Sutcliffe, who was convicted of thirteen murders committed between 1975 and 1980.

In 1974, Sutcliffe was driving around the county for work. He has been linked to four murders, including Carolyn's, in the Midlands before those he was eventually convicted of. In two of these cases, another man had a conviction overturned, like the Birmingham Six in the pub bombings. As we have seen with Michael Thornton, the police were quick to arrest on flimsy evidence, and some of the quashed convictions involved the use of false evidence or confessions obtained through coercion. Thornton, despite his long period on remand, was perhaps fortunate.

The unsolved murder usually associated with Barbara Forrest is that of Mary Ashford in 1817. Erdington's population was then under two thousand, about 10 percent of its current size. Mary was a twenty-year-old servant girl whose father, a gardener, lived at the Cross Keys public house in Erdington, another building I knew well. Mary lived with and worked for her uncle, who was a farmer in Langley Heath, now part of Walmley. In the 1980s, I traveled daily by bus to a school in Langley Heath Road along the route Mary would have followed past Pype Hayes Park. On May 26, 1817, Mary embarked on a seven-mile walk to the market in Birmingham to sell her uncle's produce. (Whitsun would not include a public holiday until 1871, when the government passed the Bank Holiday Act.)

Mary stopped on the way to Birmingham to leave some clothes with her friend, Hannah Cox, in Erdington. They had arranged to go to a dance that night at the Three Tuns public house, commonly known as the Tyburn House, which is now the official name, and the clothes were for Mary to wear. The Three Tuns was about a mile from the Bagot Arms. Bus route 67 now connects the two, though in Mary's day, people walked or rode in horse-drawn carts. She returned from the city, changed clothes, then walked to the dance with Hannah along Chester Road, possibly crossing the very spot where Barbara Forrest's body would be found 157 years later.

Also at the dance was twenty-four-year-old Abraham Thornton, an athletic man with a strong, thick neck. He was said in some accounts to be the strongest man in England, an impossible claim to verify. At Thornton's trial, a witness, John Cooke, said he heard Thornton ask a man called Cottrell who Mary was; on being told, he replied that he had been intimate with her sister and would have her too. Cottrell never gave evidence to support or deny this.

Thornton danced with Mary, whom he later recollected knowing from when she lived at The Swan, a public house on Erdington's high street, a few steps from the Cross Keys. They left the dance together around midnight, along with Hannah and her boyfriend, Benjamin Carter. Mary told Hannah that she was not going back to Erdington but instead to her grandfather's house and continued alone with Thornton. They were later seen around 3:15 a.m. in a field by a man named John Hompidge. He recognized Thornton but not Mary, who hid her face and tucked her skirts behind her.

About four in the morning, Mary returned to the house where Hannah worked as a domestic and hastily changed clothes. She said she had slept at her grandfather's house, which was later denied by the grandfather, and Thornton had gone home. Hannah noticed nothing amiss in her friend's appearance or conversation. Surprisingly, Mary kept on her dancing shoes instead of her walking boots.

At six in the morning, Mary's body was found in a pit full of water near Penns Mill in Walmley, about four hundred yards from where her grandparents lived and close to where my parents now live. Today, it is built-up, but in 1817, it was predominantly farmland, busy in the morning with laborers starting work at sunrise. An imprint of a body in the grass and congealed blood were found. A man's and a woman's footprints led up to the pit, but only the man's footprints returned. There was evidence of a chase and a scuffle, and it appeared that a couple had sex on the grass. Mary died from drowning, and there were marks on her body suggesting she had been held down. She had not eaten for at least a day. Her bonnet and shoes were placed at the side of the pit, with a bundle containing the clothes she had worn at the dance. Her dance shoes matched the female footprints.

People who had been to the dance remembered Thornton leaving with Mary. The landlord of the Three Tuns rode to the house of Thornton's father in Castle Bromwich and escorted the suspect back. Along the way, they talked about farming, and Thornton did not seem concerned about his situation even though hanging was the punishment for both murder and rape. He admitted to the landlord that he had sex with Mary and took her virginity. Bloodstains were discovered on his underwear, which he was still wearing. Mary was menstruating at the time of death. Thornton's shoes were found by witnesses to match the footprints around the pit. He was charged with the murder, then claimed he had an alibi. He said he left Erdington at about 4:10 a.m. and saw four different people on the way home. Castle Bromwich is under four miles from Erdington and eight from Walmley.

The trial took place on August 8, lasting twelve hours. The prosecution alleged that Thornton raped Mary, then threw her into the pit. Although the footprint evidence was affected by rain later in the day, the two men who examined the prints swore they saw the distinctive impressions of nails in the same pattern as on the soles of Thornton's shoes. Mary's white shoes were bloodstained, as were the white stockings and dress she had removed at Hannah's employer's house, though her black stockings, which she had changed into, were not. Thomas Dales, the constable who arrested Thornton, could not remember the details of their discussions, and the evidence he gave that Thornton voluntarily admitted to having sex with Mary was regarded as a point in Thornton's favor.

Hannah Cox said Mary arrived at the house to change at 4:40 a.m., but the clock she used was shown to be forty-one minutes fast when compared with the watch of Joseph Webster, the mill owner, who set his time by the Birmingham church clocks. Until the arrival of the railways, which reached Erdington in 1867 and Walmley in 1879, there was no common agreement on times. Webster and another mill owner, William Twamley, compared the various clocks mentioned by witnesses and attempted to standardize the times given in evidence.

A witness saw Mary after she left Hannah, walking alone in the opposite direction to Thornton. Seven people said they saw Thornton after four that morning. Erdington milkman William Jennings and his wife saw him about 4:30 a.m. John Holden, a farmer's son, and his servant Jane Heaton saw him about twenty minutes later. At 5:05 a.m., gamekeeper John Haydon had a fifteen-minute chat with Thornton. He was sure of the time because the church clock had struck five. A miller saw them talking. About ten minutes later, James Wright saw Thornton walking home. If the timings were correct, then Thornton would have had to chase and rape Mary, then carry her to the pit, throw her in, and walk three miles in less than ten minutes. He was found not guilty of murder and rape.

The local community was outraged. Rumors spread that Thornton and his father had bribed witnesses and jurors, some of whom were acquainted with the Thornton family, and even Constable Thomas Dales was sacked for misconduct. Magistrates began seeking ways to overturn the verdict.

In November 1817, a convict named Omar Hall informed the authorities that Thornton had confessed to him to the rape of Mary Ashford and the bribery of Thomas Dales while he was in Warwick jail awaiting trial. Mary apparently fainted after consensual sex and, believing she was dead, Thornton threw her in the pit. A jailer confirmed that Hall and Thornton were cellmates and that Dales visited Thornton. As a convicted felon, Hall was not allowed to give evidence in court unless he received a pardon for his own crimes. No one was willing to authorize that as there were many cases of criminals offering false information against others to obtain their freedom.

It was then impossible for a person to be tried for the same offense twice except by an obscure and ancient law known as "an appeal of murder," which dated back to Norman times. This allowed the nearest relative and heir of a murder victim to demand a second trial if there remained strong and reasonable grounds for suspecting an acquitted person of the crime. The accused had the right to respond by requesting a trial by battle, sometimes called "trial by combat."

The last known occurrence of a trial by battle was in 1446. The procedure was established as follows: A piece of ground was marked out at sunrise and a court assembled to watch. The two parties were armed with a baton or truncheon and a leather square for defense. Both had to be barefooted and bare-armed, with the accused having his head shaved. He would declare himself not guilty and throw down his glove. The accuser (prosecutor) then picked up the glove and accepted the challenge. Each swore on the Bible and declared they had no access to enchantments, sorcery, or witchcraft. They fought until the evening stars came out. If the accused could not or would not fight, he would be immediately hanged. If he died in battle, it was seen as justice being done. If he killed the prosecutor or survived until the evening, he was acquitted. If the prosecutor withdrew from battle, he had to pay compensation to the accused.

Mary's brother William Ashford was persuaded to bring an appeal against the acquittal. Thornton was rearrested and conveyed to London for his second trial. There he claimed a trial by battle on the advice of his lawyers, who believed the prejudice against him affected his right to a fair trial. Thornton's picture was in the national newspapers. On November 17, 1817, he threw down his gauntlet in Westminster Hall, declaring himself not guilty and ready to defend himself with his body.

Most people accepted that the battle was both unfair and barbaric. However, it remained on the statute books and could only be declined by a court if the accused had been caught in the act of committing the crime, attempted to escape, or the evidence of guilt was strong. None of these applied to Abraham Thornton. There were also exemptions for the accuser if he were over the age of sixty, a child, lame, blind, a peer of the realm, a priest, or a citizen of London. None of these applied to William Ashford.

The court conceded that William could either allow Thornton to go free or fight him. Knowing Thornton was physically stronger, William opted for the former, and, on April 20, 1818, Thornton was formally acquitted for the second time. In 1819, trial by battle and private appeals against criminal verdicts were abolished. The following year, Walter Scott included a trial by combat in his novel, *Ivanhoe*. The gauntlet Thornton threw down in Westminster sold at auction in 2019 for £6,875.

My research into true crime, cryptozoology, and other fields has convinced me that coincidences do exist. Sometimes these are overstated. For example, there are several websites which state that Mary Ashford and Barbara Forrest shared a birthday. We do not know the exact date when Mary was born, only that she was baptized on New Year's Eve 1897. Other sources imply a supernatural connection. In my view, it is just coincidence.

In October 1815, Ann Smith, a servant girl from Over Whitacre, about nine miles from Walmley, was found dead in a pit of water. Isaac Brindley was convicted and executed on the evidence that his shoe print and a mark where he had knelt in his corduroy breeches matched. Some features of this crime bear a closer resemblance to the death of Mary Ashford than the death of Barbara Forrest. It is also possible to argue that other murders in the 1970s resembled Barbara's case.

The only explanation, other than coincidence or supernatural influence, for the similarities between the Ashford and Forrest murders is that someone in 1974 intentionally set out to recreate the 1817 murder. To do this, they needed to either meet Barbara by agreement or wait around on the right date for a possible victim. If that was their intention, then they might be expected to find someone in Walmley, not Erdington. There were about two miles between the locations.

Barbara did not mention any meeting, and it seems unlikely she would arrange a late rendezvous in a dark park after a date with her boyfriend on the opposite side of the city. An opportunistic killer is more likely, and he couldn't have arranged for a man named Thornton to be arrested and acquitted unless he was able to influence both the police and the courts. There is no evidence of a family connection between Michael Thornton and Abraham Thornton. After his second acquittal and the national publicity, Abraham continued to be ostracized, being refused service in shops, and several ships refused to take him to the

United States. Eventually, he managed to emigrate. Unconfirmed stories indicate that he died in Baltimore in 1860.

What the two cases have in common is poor handling by the authorities. Allowances can be made for them in 1817, when there was not even an organized police force. Thomas Dales was unable to clearly remember what had been said when questioned at the trial, amid speculation that Thornton had influenced him. Certainly, it was inappropriate for a prosecution witness and member of the investigation team to visit a suspect in prison.

The comparison between the footprints and Thornton's shoes was made by members of the public, one of whom had danced with Mary on the night of her death. People crowded around the crime scene, and the medical examination was conducted on a table in a parlor by professionals who did not understand the reasons for menstruation. It is not even certain if Mary was thrown into the pit, as the marks on her body could have come from consensual sex.

In 1974, it should have been possible to ascertain how long the body had been in the ditch and whether Barbara had been killed there. This would then determine whether the police needed to look for a man with a vehicle and somewhere to hide the body or someone on foot. The arrest of Michael Thornton seems belated and desperate, based on the fact he was alleged to have had an unscheduled return to Pype Hayes Hall around the time of the murder, and the number of remands on this evidence was excessive. No other suspects are known.

In 2020, Barbara's family expressed regret that the police had not reviewed the case to consider advances in DNA evidence. Other cold cases have been solved by matching samples with modern databases. The identification of Joseph Kappen, the "Saturday Night Strangler" who killed three teenagers in South Wales in 1973, is perhaps the most famous example from the British Isles.

In 1817, Abraham Thornton was the obvious suspect. He was alone with Mary for at least an hour, and then both were seen walking in opposite directions. Mary lied about going to her grandfather's house and hid her face from the witness, John Hompidge. This suggests the encounter was after sex with Thornton, which explains the blood on his underwear. If he intended to kill Mary, he had ample opportunity before she went to see Hannah to change her clothes. He also had time to remove and hide the underwear before his arrest. His manner was seen as perfectly normal by the witnesses who spoke to him on the way home.

Either someone else was the murderer, or Thornton lurked around to deliberately ambush Mary—and every witness was lying or wrong about the times. No other suspects were ever proposed. Thornton's defense team believed Mary committed suicide due to guilt over the sex. Another possibility is that she set her bundle of clothes down to wash in the pit and fell in. She had been awake for nearly a day, not eaten in that time, drunk alcohol at the dance, lost her virginity, and walked for hours. Tired and exhausted, it is conceivable that she lost her balance.

Many of the locations, even from 1974, are considerably changed nearly half a century later. St. Mark's Lutheran Church in Birmingham has become a university chaplaincy. The Cross Keys in Erdington stands derelict, with a proposal to turn it into a homeless hostel. The Tyburn House was rebuilt in 1930 and is still a pub. There are stories that a bench outside is haunted by Mary Ashford's ghost. The Bagot Arms is derelict. Pype Hayes Hall, also said to be haunted, was the oldest occupied house in Erdington until the 1980s. It was purchased by a developer in 2015 with unrealized plans to turn it into a hotel. In September 2020, two people were saved from drowning in Pype Hayes Park in separate incidents after forty years without anyone struggling in the lake. Bus route 67 continues, with cameras installed and smart-card technology that enables the tracing of passengers. Most passengers have smartphones and the ability to provide updates on their location.

Women are safer from predatory attacks now. But I write this at a time when officials in Australia, my current home, are accused of not taking rape claims seriously, just as police and society in the late

1970s were accused of not taking seriously the women targeted by Peter Sutcliffe and other killers. The acquittal of Abraham Thornton made national news. Yet Michael Thornton's trial was not mentioned in most national newspapers.

For fifty years after her death, the grave of Mary Ashford at Holy Trinity Parish Church in Sutton Coldfield was a tourist attraction, which was aided by the arrival of the railways. Her tombstone reads:

> *As a warning to female virtue*
> *And a humble monument to female chastity,*
> *This stone marks the grave of Mary Ashford*
> *Who, in the twentieth year of her age,*
> *Having incautiously repaired to a place of amusement*
> *Without proper protection*
> *Was brutally violated and murdered*
> *On 27 May 1817.*

Despite the public support for Mary and hostility toward Abraham Thornton, the implication is that a twenty-year-old virgin contributed to her own demise by going to a dance without an escort. Such an attitude belongs in the history books, alongside trial by battle.

About the Editor

Mitzi Szereto (mitziszereto.com) is an author and anthology editor whose books span multiple genres. Her popular true crime series The Best New True Crime Stories features the volumes *Partners in Crime*; *Crimes of Passion, Obsession & Revenge*; *Well-Mannered Crooks, Rogues & Criminals*; *Small Towns*; and *Serial Killers*. She's also written crime fiction, gothic fiction, horror, cozy mystery, satire, erotic fiction, and general fiction and nonfiction. Her novels, anthologies, and short stories have been translated into several languages. She has the added distinction of being the editor of the first anthology of erotic fiction to include a Fellow of the Royal Society of Literature. Mitzi has appeared internationally on radio and television and at literature festivals and taught creative writing around the world. She produced and presented the London-based web TV channel *Mitzi TV* and portrays herself in the pseudo-documentary British film, *Lint: The Movie*. Her (oft-neglected) blog of personal essays can be found at *Errant Ramblings: Mitzi Szereto's Weblog*. The seventh volume in her true crime franchise, *The Best New True Crime Stories: Crimes of the Famous & Infamous*, will be published in 2023. She's currently working on a crime novel. Follow her on Twitter, Instagram, and TikTok @MitziSzereto.

About the Contributors

David Breakspear, whose story featured in *The Best New True Crime Stories: Well-Mannered Crooks, Rogues & Criminals*, took up creative writing in prison. After turning his life around, he now campaigns for reform in the criminal justice system in England and Wales. David's passion for prison education led to him appearing before members of Parliament to give evidence to the Education Select Committee at the House of Commons about his experiences and opinions of prison education. He lives in Kent with his partner Kelly, their two dogs Frankie and Betty, and Millie the cat.

Janel Comeau is a writer, blogger, podcaster, comedian, and human services worker currently residing in Halifax, Nova Scotia, Canada. She is a regular contributor to satire news website *The Beaverton* and cohost of the true crime podcast *Histories and Mysteries with Jessica and Janel*. Her work has previously appeared in *The Best New True Crime Stories: Well-Mannered Crooks, Rogues & Criminals*.

Ciaran Conliffe works in information security and writes about history, both pursuits that let him see the darker side of human nature. In 2013, he made a New Year's resolution to write something new every day, and he hasn't stopped since. He's best known for his long-running column "Terrible People from History" on the pop culture website *Headstuff* and has also written for numerous other publications. He enjoys public speaking and has talked about the stranger corners of history at the Workman's Club in Dublin and the Cairde Arts Festival in Sligo. He lives in Belfast, Northern Ireland.

Pamela Costello was born and raised just north of Boston. She is a teacher by day and a true crime junkie at night. Pamela currently lives in Florida with her daughter and three cats. A black belt in taekwondo, she considers sarcasm to be her native tongue and relishes any opportunity when her accent is detected to speak about her beloved city of Boston.

Lindsey Danis (lindseydanis.com) is a queer writer of fiction and essays. Her writing has appeared in *Condé Nast Traveler*, *AFAR*, *Fodor's*, and *Longreads*. Lindsey's essays have received a notable mention in *Best American Travel Writing* and are forthcoming in anthologies from PM Press, Alternating Currents Press, and elsewhere. Her work centers LGBTQ voices, with a focus on honoring LGBTQ history, celebrating queer joy, and expanding the types of queer stories that get told. When not writing, Lindsey is often found hiking or kayaking near her Hudson Valley home.

Dean Jobb (deanjobb.com) is a Canadian true crime writer whose books have won the Chicago Writers Association and Crime Writers of Canada nonfiction awards, and have been nominated for Canada's Hilary Weston Writers' Trust Prize and the American Library Association's Andrew Carnegie Medal for Excellence. He contributed to two previous The Best New True Crime Stories collections—*Well-Mannered Crooks, Rogues & Criminals* and *Crimes of Passion, Obsession & Revenge*. He writes a column on true crime for *Ellery Queen's Mystery Magazine* and teaches in the MFA in Creative Nonfiction program at the University of King's College in Halifax, Nova Scotia.

Cathy Pickens (cathypickens.com) has written crime fiction, starting with the award-winning *Southern Fried* (St. Martin's), and a regional historic true crime series, starting with *Charlotte True Crime Stories* (History Press). The latest is *Upstate South Carolina True Crime Stories*. She's served as national president of Sisters in Crime, on Mystery

Writers of America's national board, and as true crime columnist for *Mystery Readers Journal*. A lawyer and former college professor, she also wrote *CREATE! Developing Your Creative Process* (create-update.com), works with prison inmates, and coaches writers and others in creativity workshops. Her work has appeared in a previous volume of The Best New True Crime Stories series.

Deirdre Pirro, author of *Italian Sketches: The Faces of Modern Italy*, *Famous Expats in Italy*, and *Royals in Florence*, published by The Florentine Press, is an international lawyer who lives and works in Florence, Italy. She has a column in *The Florentine*, Florence's English-language newspaper, called "The Final Say." She also writes a column for the US magazine *PRIMO* entitled "The Covid Chronicles." Her stories have appeared in The Best New True Crime Stories volumes *Serial Killers*; *Small Towns*; and *Well-Mannered Crooks, Rogues & Criminals*.

C L Raven are identical twins and mistresses of the macabre. They're horror writers because "bringers of nightmares" isn't a recognized job title. They've recently switched to writing true crime and have been published in The Best New True Crime Stories volumes *Small Towns*; *Crimes of Passion, Obsession & Revenge*; and *Partners in Crime*, and are working on their first true crime book. When they're not submerged in the murky worlds of horror and true crime, they edit *When in Chrome* aerial fitness magazine, run their mobile pole studio The Pole Vault, look after their animal army, and plot to smash the patriarchy.

Iris Reinbacher settled as a writer in Kyoto, Japan, after giving up ten years of nomadic life as an academic. She most enjoys writing about all things science and technology, and features the daily mysteries of her life in Japan on her blog. Constantly curious, she is happy to explore anything new, which has led to a chapter in this book. She has also contributed the essay "Because I Loved Him" to the *Crimes of Passion, Obsession & Revenge* volume of this series.

Joan Renner, writer, social historian, and true crime expert, is the author of *The First with the Latest: Aggie Underwood, the Los Angeles Herald, and the Sordid Crimes of a City*. She contributed to the *Los Angeles Times* bestseller *LAPD '53*, written by James Ellroy and Glynn Martin. She has appeared in a previous volume of The Best New True Crime Stories. Joan lectures on historic Los Angeles crime and appears on true crime TV shows and podcasts. She is currently writing a book for University Press of Kentucky about Los Angeles during the Prohibition era.

Priscilla Scott Rhoades is the author of five novels under the pseudonym Pascal Scott (*Hard Limits, Hard Fall: A McStone and Martinelli Thriller, Hard Luck: An Elizabeth Taylor Bundy Thriller*, and *The Wife Left Behind*). For many years, she wrote for the gay and alternative press in San Francisco, including *The Sentinel* and the *San Francisco Bay Guardian*. Her short stories, poetry, and erotica have appeared in numerous publications and anthologies including *The Best New True Crime Stories: Crimes of Passion, Obsession & Revenge*. *Hard Fall* won a Golden Crown Literary Society award for best mystery in 2020.

Anya Wassenberg is a Canada-based freelance writer with a wide-ranging background in writing, covering everything from professional sports to news and the arts. In addition to freelancing as a writer and editor, she's a writing instructor at college level, and runs the long-standing *Art & Culture Maven* arts blog. It's the intersections of facts, events, and culture that have fueled her writing over a career spanning nearly three decades. Many of Anya's pieces, including posts from her blog, have been cited and appear in the bibliographies of academic publications, periodicals, and other media.

Paul Williams is the author of three nonfiction books, including an award-winning guide to Jack the Ripper suspects, and sixty-five short stories, plus articles, reviews, and poetry. This is his fourth contribution to The Best New True Crime Stories series.

Mango Publishing, established in 2014, publishes an eclectic list of books by diverse authors—both new and established voices—on topics ranging from business, personal growth, women's empowerment, LGBTQ studies, health, and spirituality to history, popular culture, time management, decluttering, lifestyle, mental wellness, aging, and sustainable living. We were recently named 2019 *and* 2020's #1 fastest growing independent publisher by *Publishers Weekly.* Our success is driven by our main goal, which is to publish high quality books that will entertain readers as well as make a positive difference in their lives. Our readers are our most important resource; we value your input, suggestions, and ideas. We'd love to hear from you—after all, we are publishing books for you!

Please stay in touch with us and follow us at:

Facebook: Mango Publishing
Twitter: @MangoPublishing
Instagram: @MangoPublishing
LinkedIn: Mango Publishing
Pinterest: Mango Publishing
Newsletter: mangopublishinggroup.com/newsletter

Join us on Mango's journey to reinvent publishing, one book at a time.

CPSIA information can be obtained
at www.ICGtesting.com
Printed in the USA
BVHW041219261222
654958BV00018B/1081